THE PAST IS AN IMPERFECT TENSE

T0153239

Praise for this book

'Like Kucinski's first novel, K, this is a powerful evocation of parental love and loss. *The Past is an Imperfect Tense* juxtaposes scattered memories, retrospective regrets and scientific research as the narrator looks back over his son's life and tries to piece together what went wrong.'

Claire Williams, Associate Professor of Brazilian Literature and Culture at the University of Oxford

'This is first and foremost the compelling, relentlessly honest account of a parent's agonised battle to love, understand and support an adopted son seemingly lost to drug dependency. But Kucinski tells that story by moving between Brazil and Israel, against a background of anti-black racism, social and political brutality, the migrant Arab diaspora experience, and the plight of the Palestinians. And in so doing he manages to suggest, subtly but powerfully, how his traumatised characters struggle to survive as a family, to come to terms with the scars of abandonment, deception, prejudice and guilt, might also stand for a broader condition of exile and precarity in our contemporary world.'

David Treece, Camoens Professor of Portuguese at King's College London

The Past is an Imperfect Tense

Bernardo Kucinski

translated by Tom Gatehouse
with drawings by Enio Squeff

The Past is an Imperfect Tense was first published in English in 2020 by Practical Action Publishing Ltd and Latin America Bureau

Practical Action Publishing Ltd
27a Albert Street, Rugby, Warwickshire, CV21 2SG, UK
www.practicalactionpublishing.org

Latin America Bureau,
Enfield House, Castle Street, Clun, Shropshire, SY7 8JU, UK
www.lab.org.uk

ISBN 978-1-78853-087-3 Paperback
ISBN 978-1-78853-088-0 Hardback
ISBN 978-1-78853-089-7 Epub
ISBN 978-1-78853-090-3 PDF

Since 1974, Practical Action Publishing has published and disseminated books and information in support of international development work throughout the world. Practical Action Publishing is a trading name of Practical Action Publishing Ltd (Company Reg. No. 1159018), the wholly owned publishing company of Practical Action. Practical Action Publishing trades only in support of its parent charity objectives and any profits are covenanted back to Practical Action (Charity Reg. No. 247257, Group VAT Registration No. 880 9924 76).

Latin America Bureau (Research and Action) Limited is a UK registered charity (no. 1113039). Since 1977 LAB has been publishing books, news, analysis and information about Latin America, reporting consistently from the perspective of the region's poor, oppressed or marginalized communities and social movements. In 2015 LAB entered into a publishing partnership with Practical Action Publishing.

The views and opinions in this publication are those of the author and do not represent those of Practical Action Publishing Ltd or its parent charity Practical Action or of Latin America Bureau (Research and Action) Limited. Reasonable efforts have been made to publish reliable data and information, but the authors and publishers cannot assume responsibility for the validity of all materials or for the consequences of their use.

Product or corporate names may be trademarks or registered trademarks, and are used only for identification and explanation without intent to infringe.

A catalogue record for this book is available from the British Library.
A catalogue record for this book has been requested from the Library of Congress.

Citation: Kucinski, Bernardo (2020) *The Past is an Imperfect Tense,* Rugby, UK: Practical Action Publishing, http://dx.doi.org/10.3362/9781788530903

Cover illustration by Enio Squeff
Cover design by RCO.Design
Printed in the UK
Typeset by vPrompt eServices Pvt. Ltd.

 MINISTÉRIO DA CIDADANIA
Fundação BIBLIOTECA NACIONAL   MINISTÉRIO DA
CIDADANIA   

This work was first published in Portuguese with the support of the National Library Foundation and Ministry of Citizenship

Obra publicada com o apoio da Fundação Biblioteca Nacional | Ministério da Cidadania

 ENGLISH PEN    Supported using public funding by **ARTS COUNCIL ENGLAND**

This book has been selected to receive financial assistance from English PEN's Writers in Translation programme supported by Bloomberg and Arts Council England. English PEN exists to promote literature and its understanding, uphold writers' freedoms around the world, campaign against the persecution and imprisonment of writers for stating their views, and promote the friendly co-operation of writers and free exchange of ideas.

www.englishpen.org

Acknowledgments

I owe a considerable debt to those who read my original manuscript and made very helpful suggestions. To all these, my thanks: Enio Squeff, Julián Fuks, Leila Lapyda, Lilia Schwarcz, Luiz Schwarcz, Maria Rita Kehl, Otávio Marques da Costa, Reinaldo Morano, Ricardo Teperman, Toni Cotrim and Wanda Gomes. To my wife, Mutsuko, and to my son, Elias, my thanks for supporting this publication.

For Jonas and Elias

Le temps d'apprendre à vivre il est déjà trop tard
[The time for learning how to live, is already too late]

Louise Aragon, Poèmes

All sorrows can be borne if you put them into a story or tell a story
about them

Isak Dinesen, interview
The New York Times Book Review

1.

I'll start at the end: with the letter. I wrote it by hand, weighing my every word. I sent it the old-fashioned way: a postman, a knock at the door, via recorded delivery, to be sure of it reaching the intended recipient. I included no return address. It needed no response.

I won't repeat what I wrote in its entirety. They weren't kind things to say, nothing that I'm proud of. But I had no choice.

The figure of the father who casts his son from the home has always existed. God banished man from paradise, His home, even though man was His son, created in His own image. The founding myth, paradise forever lost. But while God punished the first sin, I let countless sins go unpunished. It took me a long time to come to the letter. It was a thirty-year learning process, father learning from son, with each lesson more painful than the last. Finally, tired of fretting every time the phone rang, tired of getting my hopes up only to see them dashed again and again, I decided to disown him once and for all, my only son. I banished him out of exhaustion.

My letter was a kind rejection. The Japanese, when dealing with feckless children, put a backpack on their shoulders and send them out into

1

the world. These children become drifters, and wherever they go, people give them something to eat. But the intention isn't to punish, and neither was mine. I didn't even expel him from the house as such. He had been living far away for more than ten years, the other side of the ocean. It's true, he had left in a hurry, hoping in other lands to abandon the frenzied pursuit of an artificial paradise. It wasn't about excluding him from our family life, but from within me. I could only achieve that by rationalising things. Hence the idea of the letter, to banish him from my affections in writing; arguing, not shouting. A solemn letter. An epistle.

I told him that we had never imposed a future on him, as some parents do, though inevitably when he was growing up he must have construed certain ideas from our words and actions. Most of all, we just wanted him to be a good person. We weren't concerned about the little virtues of temperament, like prudence or modesty, nor innate attributes like intelligence or dexterity, but values related to conscience and the will, unique to the individual. Moral values to help him distinguish good from bad in each situation and act accordingly. Simply put, we wanted him to be a man of character.

I explained that though our ancestors came from very different backgrounds, they were all honourable people. There were times they were silent, I wrote, because what they had to say couldn't be said – but they didn't lie. Sometimes they cried, but they never shed pointless tears. Sometimes they weren't strong enough, but they did no evil. They didn't always have enough food to satisfy their hunger, but they never refused a place at the table to the stranger who came knocking at the door.

In our family, I wrote, we've never failed to keep a promise, settle a debt, or meet an obligation. In our family, we never blame each other, not even at the most bitter moments. Most importantly, in our family we don't steal, we don't betray our friends, and we don't raise our hands to women. These are things we never do, I told him, but you have done them all.

You excluded yourself from our family years ago, I wrote. You've been running into trouble for years, not just once or twice, and not just because you were careless. You've been arrested and convicted. I've also been to prison, and I had to go into exile, just like my father before me. But not for selfish motives: we were resisting tyranny. I have been naïve, I concluded. I hadn't realised I was torturing myself for no good reason, because a son with whom I had nothing in common could be no son of mine.

A pathetic letter? Perhaps. But what else could I do? I realised, all of a sudden, that I had become an old man. And I'd been struck by an awareness of how little time I had left. The letter was an emancipation that had been a long time coming. My own.

2.

I don't identify at all with that letter, with all that resentment, that bitterness; on the contrary, when I close my eyes and think of him, what I see is a sweet, affectionate child. I'm going to tell you something you don't know, because I was the one who used to pick him up from creche. As soon as he saw me, he would come running up, and once he got close he would start dancing for joy. I would look around at the other children with their mums and their grandmas, some of them happy, others grouchy, but in him I only saw contentedness, joy. It was his rite of celebration for my arrival. Isn't that sweet? What joie de vivre *... Since he was little, even before he could walk, his eyes shone with happiness. He would begin playing as soon as he woke; a hunk of bread would be a car, a pebble dangling from a piece of string an aeroplane. Soon he wanted to go to school, and he was the one who asked; he would say, "Mum, isn't it time I went to school?" He wanted to be the first one there. He enjoyed being at home, he enjoyed being at school, he enjoyed every second, and yet he was in no hurry, there was no rush. I found it curious; he had at the same time the vivacity of a child and the serenity of a wise old man. Isn't that interesting? And he was such a bold little boy. Such willpower and determination! I remember the day he threw his baby bottle away;*

4

he wouldn't hear of drinking from it again. And the first time he stood up? He still had plaster on his legs. He grasped the rails of his cot, roared like a samurai, and pulled himself up in one go. He was always determined like that. And do you remember how he used to sit down to eat? He looked like an aristocrat. That was something that really struck me; even when he was little, he used a knife and fork without putting his elbows on the table. He didn't learn that from you. And what an appetite! He would eat anything; he wasn't fussy at all. He hardly ever complained. And his friends? Don't you remember how easily he made friends? Wherever he went, he would make a friend. He was a charming boy. I never saw him sulky or sad, not until he was a teenager. Not until the problems started. That's how I remember him affectionate, at ease with life. Things may have turned out the way they did, but there's no way he's this lowlife you make him out to be in your letter, and he never has been. Even less so a psychopath. I wouldn't have written a letter like that. I'm not saying it was unfair; everyone has their own way of expressing themselves. But what I want to express is how much he gave me, not how much he took away.

3.

1979 was a memorable year. The Shah of Iran was overthrown in January, and the Nicaraguan dictator Somoza in July. In Brazil, the dictatorship's grip on power was weakening. In September, I screened my short film about the Cabanagem uprising at a documentary film festival in New York. There was also a talk on Cinema and Revolution, where I met the Druze Abou al-Walid, famous for his films of the Palestinian conflict in which the camera participates in the action, the lens being the gaze of a protestor.

With his square face, straight nose, and bushy eyebrows, Abou reminded me of my Lebanese grandfather, with whom I used to spend holidays in Manaus. Abou and I discovered we shared some ideas, and not only about cinema. We were the same age too. We got on so well that we mapped out then and there the idea for a documentary on the Palestinian diaspora in Brazil. The Palestinian peasant, Abou explained, is every bit as rooted in his plot of land as the hundred-year-old olive trees that sustain him, which are passed down through the family, generation to generation. Exile is therefore doubly painful: as well as being cut off from an abstract homeland, the Palestinians feel nostalgia for their ancestral space and the villages within it, the lands of their childhood. I would film in Brazil, and Abou in the Arab villages in Israel, where he lived, and in the West Bank.

I was due to cover the Sandinista victory in Nicaragua as soon as the event in New York was over. That was the plan. Two weeks out of Brazil. I was thinking about Nicaragua whilst watching Ricardo Costa's *April Carnations* with Abou, when someone tapped me on the shoulder. "A call from Brazil", they whispered. My wife wouldn't phone without good reason. An accident perhaps? I always imagine the worst. "There's a baby, what do you think?" she said, as soon as I came to the phone. Right now? "I have to decide today", she said. I could tell from the flutter in her voice that she had already made up her mind and was only phoning for encouragement. "Boy or girl?" I asked. "A boy, a chubby little thing." I realised that she had already seen the baby, fallen for him, set her heart on him. "Yes, fine", I said. "Can you take care of things until I get back?" "Yes, don't worry."

There were still no direct flights to Nicaragua. But I had been fired up by the Sandinista Revolution and I was absolutely determined to get to Managua. I had planned a ten-part documentary, a new *Ten Days That Shook the World*. Direct cinema, in the heat of the moment. I would film like Abou, with the camera on my shoulders, shooting a sequence per day. I managed to get as far as Tegucigalpa, the capital of Honduras, from where the first flights were going to Managua after weeks of disruption. That was where I filmed the first scene, as I was buying my ticket. The dialogue I wrote, short and emblematic, was a riff on a passage from the chronicle *Man's Hope*, by Malraux. As I spelt out the S, I said *S de Sandino! No de Somoza, un hijo de puta ... de Sandino, querida*. I felt inspired.

Managua resembled the surface of the moon, devastated not only by the civil war, but also the earthquake of 1972. Here and there were the mansions of rich families who had fled to Miami. It wasn't easy to film enough to put together a sequence per day. I worked frenetically, from early morning until the last glimmer of sunlight disappeared. Then I would immerse myself in the script and the map of locations for the next day's filming. I had completely forgotten that I had just become a father.

4.

What did we know about adoption? Nothing, absolutely nothing. Almost a lifetime later, when what had been done couldn't be undone, I decided to study the issue. Today I do know something about it, though not a great deal. A handful of ideas fished from an ocean of problems. It gave me a shock.

Common sense dictates that adoption is an act of charity. What rubbish! People almost always adopt in order to have a family, not to provide the child with one. It's our own wretchedness that motivates us, not the greater wretchedness of the child. People adopt to escape grief, to make up for a loss, to save a marriage – or a combination of the above.

Some people adopt just to make sure they'll be looked after in old age. Even in informal adoptions by relatives or neighbours due to death or incapacity, there may be ulterior motives. Whatever the reason, adoption is possession, acquisition. In unofficial adoption, what we call *adoção à brasileira*, sometimes money even changes hands, to cover expenses involved in the birth. In orphanages, couples pick out the child they think the prettiest, as if choosing the colour of a new car. Until recently, an adopted child could be registered with a public notary the same way one registers property.

According to the adoption scholar Eduardo Sá, this is how things are everywhere. And it's always been this way, since time immemorial. In antiquity, childless couples adopted to ensure the essential rite of the veneration of their souls after death. They were thinking of themselves, of their own afterlives, not the child's misfortune. With Catholicism, adoption became a means of preserving patrimony, as the Church appropriated property for which there was no heir. That's why the Church opposed adoption, selling the children it received into slavery or putting them in the service of the priests.

In the work of Michel Soulé, a French psychoanalyst, I discovered the concept of narcissistic injury, a motive for adoption buried deep in our unconscious. The inability to conceive – associated with both male sexual impotence and the ancient stigma of the barren woman – humiliates us, producing narcissistic injury. In turning the dream of a family to dust, it degrades man and woman alike. Soulé writes of the traumatic impact of an infertility diagnosis.

And the risks of adoption? What did we know of the risks? The same: nothing. We didn't bother talking to people who had adopted, nor did we do any research. How does one compose the narrative of an adoption for the adopted child? What does the stigmatizing expression "adopted child" mean for them? Where do they fit into the genealogy, the family psyche? And how does all of this affect our own psyche?

Not one of these questions even crossed our minds. Having read the French philosopher Pierre Levy, I now know that every adoption is a foolhardy act. You were brave, our friends used to say. Another misconception! If we knew nothing of the risks, nor of anything else, then we weren't brave: we were foolish. That's right. We were irresponsible.

The longing for children can have deep roots. In early childhood we play house, assuming the roles of mother and father. In adulthood, this becomes the search for some kind of eternity, through passing on our physical characteristics and our family names. We hadn't the slightest idea about any of these reasons. We had only a vague desire for completeness. We wanted a child to complete us.

5.

*I don't like this discharge in his eyes one bit. Put him on his back. That's right ...
Undress him slowly, nice and slow, I want to see his belly button. Hmm ... Just
as I thought ... It's also discharging pus and it's not an infection of the stump,
it's coming from within, like in his eyes ... This isn't good news ... Do you know
who the parents are? I'm asking because it could be syphilis; it's very common in
babies given up for adoption, dormant syphilis, transmitted through the placenta.
Let's see his legs. Unroll everything ... More ... More ... All the way. Hmm ...
Bowed tibias. We call this tibia vara. It's fairly common, but I've never seen such
a severe case. Nor so symmetrical. This is very serious. The symmetry suggests
an organic cause, possibly rickets. If it's rickets, then that explains the discharge
from his eyes and belly button. That means it's not syphilis, though these diag-
noses often come together. It's a question of poverty – terrible poverty and great
ignorance. A lack of basic hygiene precautions, a lack of knowledge. It's best if it's
rickets rather than syphilis, because in adulthood dormant syphilis can lead to
madness ... Well, in rare cases anyway. The most common symptoms are marks
on the skin and hair loss. What happens if it's rickets? That depends on the
severity. In general, the child will be shorter. The cause? Simply put, it's hunger.*

The mother of this baby probably went hungry, compromising the development of the foetus. The bones become porous and break easily. As I said, the bowing is severe. Even if he isn't suffering from severe malnutrition – we call it protein-energy malnutrition – he'll still need to have his legs in plaster for quite some time. How long? You'd have to ask an orthopaedist, but I reckon two or three months, and afterwards he'll have to use an orthopaedic aid until his legs straighten. What's protein-energy malnutrition? It's when the lack of nutrients is so severe that the body feeds itself from its own tissues. It consumes the muscles, and the entire body atrophies, and then there's no solution, there's no point in trying to feed, because the child loses the capacity to absorb nutrients, as well as losing certain antibodies and suffering from diarrhoea. It can even cause mental retardation. We call this marasmus ... You know, those children with the lost gaze, who barely move ... That's quite right, just like the babies in Biafra, except there it's because of premature weaning, when another child is born and the mother abandons the one that was born first. As this boy has only just been born, that's not the case. He lacked nutrients in the womb. And it must have been really bad, because nature ensures the nutrition of the foetus even if the mother goes hungry. I suspect his mother tried to hide her pregnancy. What if it's marasmus? We'll only know that after blood tests and x-rays. It's going to be tough. I'll be frank: half of all babies with marasmus don't live longer than a week or two. And of those that survive, many will never be healthy children. My advice? Give him back! Give him back, as fast as you can, before you get too attached.

6.

The garden became a sea of little white flags. Nappies, nappies, nappies. We had to put up endless washing lines so we could hang them all up. A diarrhoeic baby. What's more, allergic to disposable nappies. The plastic left his skin inflamed. They had to be soft cotton nappies. His mother would carefully select the most delicate cotton fabric, cut it into rectangular pieces sixty centimetres wide, and then rinse them in water to make them even softer.

And how he shat! Piles and piles of it, nauseating, viscous. His organism wasn't absorbing nutrients properly, meaning that he ate a lot and shat just as much. A complication from the rickets, that was the explanation. At nursery, his appetite caused consternation. He would have seconds, then eat again once he got home. It was as if he were trying to make up for those nine months of deprivation he suffered whilst in the womb.

His mother soon developed a strategy to deal with so much shit. With her nose covered, she would dangle the nappies in the toilet bowl and pull the chain. Then she'd leave them to soak in a bucket for two days, with coconut soap. Only then would she wash them, one by one, hanging them out on the line to bleach in the sun. To clean his bottom, she always had a cotton rag and a two-litre thermos flask filled with hot water to hand. This was how things were until he was two years old, though by the time he was a year and a half he wouldn't allow his nappy to be changed when other people were present. He was bashful, even from a young age.

7.

"See if there's a dark mark in the cuticle of his nail", said the rude attendant. "What type of mark?" I asked. "A stripe", she said. Then she opened his hand, and there it was. "He's going to be black", she said, a look of disgust on her face. The world was revealing itself to him, though he hadn't been in it for long. He must have been six months old, if that.

I don't understand how certain people know so much. Soon afterwards, his complexion darkened and his hair became curly. By the time he was four, he was a little mulatto. That was when he had a fight with the boy next door, whose mother chased him away. "You're an orphan", she said, "Who knows who your mother was!" He came up the stairs sobbing, tripping over every step. Words can hurt more than a dagger, leaving marks that never heal.

Some people deliberately adopt children of other ethnicities, a Vietnamese orphan or a black baby, to make it clear that the child is adopted. Or to make sure that the child can't be confused with the imaginary baby that they so desired, but couldn't have, or with the child that they had, but lost.

We knew nothing of that. We would have preferred him to look a little like one of us, so as to avoid the constant questions and curious looks. But it didn't work out that way. As he grew, we became proud of the obvious incongruence. Me, the son of Lebanese immigrants, with a rectangular face and Caucasian features, and dark eyes and hair. My wife, the daughter of Bessarabian Jews, with a long face and Slavic features, blonde corkscrew curls, and blue eyes. And then him, a mulatto with tightly curled hair.

8.

In the fervent search for their mother's breast, adopted children find only the fake teat of a baby bottle. Their whole world begins with a fraud. The bogus mother then tries to make up for this injustice by lavishing them with special tenderness, which they accept. Newborns have a formidable capacity to adapt. Even so, the fraud will leave scars. How so? Well, I've studied this too, and I was shocked by the implications of such an apparently innocent crime. The one which most surprised me was identified by the renowned English psychoanalyst Wilfred Bion, who believed that the newborn's search for the mother's breast is more than just its first vital instinct: it's also its first intellectual exercise. Why? Because to think, according to Bion, is to process a pre-existing idea. The baby thinks of the breast before seeking it. But it thinks of a swollen, milky nipple, not a plastic teat. So the fraud is intellectual as well. Bion believed that if the baby were unable to overcome the frustration stemming from this falsehood, its capacity to process thought may be permanently weakened by a tendency to flee from reality. It's a frightening theory! At first, I thought it was purely speculative, based on Freud and Melanie Klein. But then

I discovered modern neurology, which studies electrical signals in the brain and its reaction to stimuli. According to the neurologists, the brain retains traces of trauma forever – even those experienced in the womb – the same way an archaeological site retains traces of ancient civilizations. And the traumatic memory, even the most remote, will interfere with present behaviour.

We also had to keep his legs in plaster for two months to correct his bowed tibias. That's another traumatic memory, because the child acquires its first perceptions of what is permitted and what is forbidden through the movement of its own body. From the very moment a person's life begins, it exists within the body. Even after the plaster came off, for another year he had to have his legs fixed to irons attached to his boots, restricting his movement.

He seemed not to mind. He soon discovered a way of crawling, wiggling his back from one side to the other, and could even stand up, using his own body to provide impetus. But I do wonder whether the leg irons left him with a greater sense of ontological insecurity than that which is natural for humans.

Nearly forty years later, we still have the leg irons, with the boots. We kept them as a memento. Once a month we took him to see Dr Andreucci, the old Italian orthopaedist who had designed them, who was able to recognise whatever was crooked or out of place using touch alone. "Aren't you going to take x-rays?" we once asked him. "No", he shot back. "This boy will have a lot of x-rays in his life, there's no need for me to start now."

9.

He had a high fever for twelve days. His nose ran; his eyes wept. His breathing became heavy. His brow was constantly damp. Fits of vomiting shook his tiny body. If he managed to swallow a little milk or broth, it would go straight through him. He was being consumed by fever. He couldn't sleep. We thought he was going to die. He was so hot that his body burnt his mother's arms. She kept a vigil at his side, trying to bring his temperature down with cold compresses.

Every other day she would wrap him in a blanket and take him to the homeopath, who could give us nothing to bring down the fever. Even so, he didn't cry. Beneath his swollen eyelids, his eyes flared with the will to live. On the thirteenth day, his mother played him one of Handel's symphonies. Little by little, the fever retreated. He closed his eyes and slept. Then his mother slept. We all slept. He was nine months old.

10.

I met my wife in Belém do Pará, during the making of my film about the Cabanagem revolt. An anthropologist, she was interested in the indigenous cause and was a researcher at the Emílio Goeldi Museum. We fell in love instantly, and two months later we were married. We didn't want to wait long before having children, but the years went by and she didn't get pregnant. If she had, we would never have adopted. Simple as that.

Even so, we didn't have to adopt. Adopting meant definitively admitting our failure to conceive. We had undergone long and gruelling tests, which failed to determine who was to blame. Or rather, what was the cause. As if either of us could be blamed. As if a biological flaw implied a moral flaw, for which we had to be punished by the fertility goddesses.

We were also going through a lot of grief. These were the darkest years of the dictatorship, a time when we lost various friends and family members. We needed some form of recompense. Some reparation for lost affection. At weekends we would get together in the countryside, at the house of one or another of our friends, their children playing while we, the adults, sipped beer and exchanged information in whispers. Then the opportunity arose, and without hesitating, without even thinking, we adopted.

11.

You haven't said a word about his umbilical hernia. Don't you remember? It was so big it looked like a penis. Big and ugly. And he had phimosis. The doctor had told us it was best to operate before he was a year and a half, and he was a year and four months. I had been scared by Andreucci's warning that he would need surgery on his knee, and since dealing with the phimosis and the umbilical hernia were simple procedures, we took him to the Hospital do Servidor to save money. Do you remember? You were going to film somewhere and had to catch a flight, so you left me at the entrance. When you came back, it had all been taken care of very nicely. But I never told you what happened. It was easy enough getting him admitted. There was a massive queue, but he was agitated and wouldn't keep quiet. In the end he made such a racket that they let me go to the front. He was admitted the same day. They told me they would operate the next day, but that I couldn't stay there. So I went home, but when I went back early the next morning the doctor said they couldn't operate because his chest was full of phlegm. They couldn't give him anaesthetic. They told me to take him home, wait for his chest to clear, and bring him back a couple of days later. I did as I was told. But then his chest filled up with phlegm again and they couldn't operate.

That was when they realised it might be some kind of allergic reaction, either to the hospital or the bedsheets. So they decided to put him in an oxygen tent. Only then did they operate. They did the umbilical hernia and the phimosis at the same time. When he came round from the anaesthetic I was at his side. I remember putting my hand in the oxygen tent. He grabbed it as hard as he could and stood up in bed and soon enough he was wandering round the hospital corridors. They kept him in for two days, for observation. By that point he had charmed the doctors, the nurses, the cleaners, everyone. And he loved the hospital. When he heard the rattle of the food trolley, he would run ahead to get his tray. He would ask for seconds, and they served him with pleasure, as if he were their own child. You should have seen it. "Look how well it turned out", said Flávio, the doctor, proudly holding the boy's willy: "like the work of a plastic surgeon". It was tough when we got home though: it hurt him to pee; he would pee and cry at the same time. You should have told the story of the phimosis and the umbilical hernia. I thought it was going to be so easy. But it was a saga.

12.

I analyse a photo in search of answers. He's standing on the bonnet of a Volkswagen Beetle with his arms raised and his fists closed in a gesture of triumph, like a boxer who has just knocked out his opponent. His eyes, which are almost closed, show intense joy. His cheeks – bulging like those of a trumpet player – and his slightly raised chin give him a mocking air.

He's four years old. I consult Piaget: at this age, the child is the centre of the world; that's how they want to be seen. They ask constant questions and tell endless stories in which reality and fantasy intermingle. The photo is typical of those parents are always taking of their children. They're an expression of affection, perhaps also of a secret desire for control through the continuous monitoring of their lives. The photo camera as security camera. The images come together to form a coherent narrative of family life, and can even foreshadow the undesirable.

In this photo his head is enormous, completely out of proportion to his rachitic frame; it's as if it had been taken from someone else and stuck on his body with a stake. It also recalls a scarecrow: amusing, but grotesque. And just like a scarecrow, he's wearing little in the way of clothing, just a boatneck T-shirt and a pair of shorts. He's barefoot. His complexion is chocolate brown. In the background, you can see the undergrowth and the perforated wall of our beach house. We had just built it specially so we could enjoy holidays on the beach whenever we had a few days off work, and he could breathe clean air.

Our house was one of the first in that development. The beach was perfect for kids: exceptionally long and gently sloping. It was deserted back then. Between the house and the sea there was a patch of Atlantic forest followed by a vast reed bed. In the absence of any other houses or street lighting, the nights were stunning, the Milky Way visible in all its splendour. From the terrace, the intermittent croaking of toads could be heard above the endless murmur of the waves. Every now and then, our little garden was invaded by clouds of fireflies.

The shadows suggest the photo was taken late afternoon. Piaget says that at age four the child begins to perceive danger and feel anger and frustration. This isn't what the photo shows. In his expression there is not a trace of fear, nor of disappointment. The moment captured is one of pure joy. He poses for the camera with the stance of someone set to conquer the world. He is, quite simply, a happy boy.

13.

When he was very small, I would carry him up the steep flight of steps that led into the house. He would hold onto me for dear life, his hands clasped around my neck, his legs wrapped around my waist, his little body fastened tight to mine. The image that came to mind was a baby monkey clinging to its mother, like you see on BBC documentaries. Today, a different image springs to mind: the victim of a shipwreck, clinging to a lifebuoy with the last of their strength. And yet it wasn't a desperate or clumsy embrace. It was as if he were part of my body. I didn't even feel his weight.

Once, when we were almost at the top of the steps, I gave him a few smacks on the bum. I can't remember why. But I remember doing it to this day, along with the remorse I felt, because I smacked him hard, and I was scared I might have broken his bones, he was so weak. This memory – which I've never shared with my wife – best reflects my view of him as a fragile child, with bones prone to shattering, as if made of glass.

On another occasion – though I was ashamed of the thought – it even occurred to me he had bad blood, an unconscious trace of the doctor's hypothesis of dormant syphilis. Whenever he hurt himself, his blood would take a long time to clot. Because of the boots and leg irons, wounds opened up between his toes which took a long time to heal. One weekend, his right foot developed festering sores and went totally purple. It looked like necrosis. I remember being terrified. Not long before that, the father of a close friend had died from a necrotic leg. We were on our way to the beach, but with difficulty we managed to find a paediatrician, who calmed us down, explaining that the purplish colouring was due to traces of his black ethnicity. He reassured us that it wasn't necrosis, in spite of its startling appearance. He was right: in a few days, the wounds closed and the purplish colouring disappeared. His foot healed completely.

Why am I recalling these episodes? Why include my wife's account about the operation on the phimosis and hernia, for which I was barely present and which I didn't even remember? It's to understand the nature of our attachment: parenthood without the history of a pregnancy, which from the beginning affects the man emotionally and completely transforms the woman, making her more emotional and sensitive.

An expectant mother and the foetus form a single body, sharing fluids, moods, and cognitive sensations. And what about the growing trepidation? Because for human beings, giving birth is no picnic. It's rupture. "In pain shall you bring forth children", says God to Eve in Genesis. Unconsciously, the mother regresses to her own experiences as a baby, her own store of memories. That's another reason maternity is risky. There's a risk of post-natal depression. A risk of psychotic episodes. A risk of succumbing to the extreme of rejecting the baby. At birth, the body of the mother breaks in two, and the baby emerges into the world as a new being, but the two parts remain emotionally united, whether by love or the lack of it.

Our attachment had none of this. Neither for good nor bad. There was no body that split in two, no prior emotional fusion. There was no risk of post-natal depression nor rejection of the baby. Our attachment was born uncomplicated, because the adopted child is necessarily desired, longed for, and sought out. But it was born in shock, in the moment of a hasty adoption. And it was gradually woven out of care and concern, as if we were looking after a fragile plant that was at risk of perishing. It was forged from our almost daily pilgrimages to paediatricians, homeopaths, and orthopaedists. Then later, much later, it turned into something comprised of psychologists' appointments and fear. Especially fear.

14.

This is a story with neither beginning nor end. It has no beginning, because despite everything I now know, I still can't say for certain at which point exactly and for what reasons he launched himself into the insane pursuit of an artificial paradise, which quickly became a hell. There's something in this story that I can't grasp. There are details which elude me, even fundamental ones. I keep thinking about whether it happened suddenly, or whether it was a gradual process. Whether it started in childhood, with the first stabs of prejudice and racism, or in adolescence, when the child acquires self-awareness and, with it, feelings of worry and angst.

Would it have been possible, at any point, to change the course of this story? Or was it all destined to be? *Maktub!* Nothing to be done! Like other stories, this has a finite number of characters. Apart from him, his mum, dad, a few friends. Not many. And a limited supporting cast. Doctors, police officers, neighbours. The action is extensive in both space and time. It spans three continents, and may have begun in the womb of his biological mother, who for reasons we will never know, could not keep him and gave him up as soon as she brought him into the world.

The ancients believed that pregnant women were especially impression-able. Any disturbance that they felt would affect the soul of the unborn child. Today we no longer talk of belief, nor the soul, but we know that pregnant women pass down their vices and eating habits to their children, as well as some purely cognitive sensations. Geneticists call them epigenetic marks, because they influence the character of the child, though they don't form part of the mother's DNA.

Just as I don't know how the story began, I don't know how it will end. I do know that I won't feature in the ending. I quit, out of self-preservation. One character less. Now I'm just a narrator, a little helpless, a little sad. The story might end worse than it stands today, or by some miracle or twist of fate, it might have a happy ending, like an American film.

No. I lie. It can't end like an American film, because part of the damage is irreversible. According to the psychiatrist Bruce Perry, chemical dependence leaves an indelible scar in the brain – especially when there has been childhood trauma. And nor can lost time be recovered. Half a life. What remains is the hope that it stays at that.

15.

Upon returning from his first day at primary school, he knew the names of all the other boys and girls in his class and what each of them was like; he had discovered who led and who followed; he had sussed out the groups and who was in charge; he knew whom he could trust and from whom he had to defend himself. I was struck not only by his phenomenal memory, but also his ability to perceive the dynamics of a collective after just one chaotic and confusing encounter. He seemed motivated by a warning instinct that was almost animal. As if he had felt vulnerable in a predatory world from a very young age. He was seven years old.

16.

Then came the feedback: he's not interested: he doesn't pay attention. This was odd; after all, he was a lively, bright boy. At first we blamed the teachers. A bunch of incompetents. His mother began to help him with his homework. She taught him his times tables, how to multiply and divide, a little grammar. He learnt quickly, but if she put any pressure on him or demanded any extra effort, he immediately stopped paying attention. He would switch off, like when a breaker cuts a circuit due to a power surge.

We worked out that the problem wasn't just at school. There was something wrong with him. A specialist diagnosed attention deficit disorder, which is common in children and adolescents but disappears in adulthood. Today I know that adopted children tend to speculate about their biological mothers precisely at moments of learning. They switch off. It's as if one question triggers another, and then another, until they arrive at the bigger question, which, though it might lie dormant, never leaves them: why were they adopted?

Some years later, when he was a teenager, he wouldn't compete in sporting events – though he was one of the strongest swimmers, and his coaches would urge him to do so. Same story for the school plays at the end of the year, when he would refuse to play the guitar. I interpreted this as modesty, or even as a sign of his good character. He took no pleasure in defeating an opponent, nor would he succumb to vanity. Today, I interpret it differently. It's as if he felt like a stowaway on the ship of existence, an illegal traveller, a fare dodger who had to hide until the end of the journey.

17.

I found a bundle of photographs of him in which no traces of the rickets can be seen. He had become handsome, a fine figure of a boy. But in almost all of them, he seems melancholic. Had he lost his *joie de vivre* so early? He had certainly lost something. In the photo which most caught my eye, he's sitting beside his mother on a bench in the garden, holding a toy arrow. His expression is serious, his eyes fixed on the ground. His mother seems sunk in gloomy thoughts; her expression is one of tragedy. What can have happened?

At the beach once, he got into an argument with another boy, whose mother then called him a criminal, a filthy half-caste. Another time, at a shopping centre, he was waiting for his mother outside a shop when a security guard took him for a thief and hauled him off to a dingy back room. After that, he avoided going even to the little neighbourhood market alone. Could it be that the conversation captured in the photograph related to one such episode? And they only became more frequent as he got older. He would often get pulled over by the police when driving his mother's car. Once, he was standing by the car, waiting for her outside a doctor's surgery, when two officers came out of nowhere, guns drawn. They forced him to stand spread-eagled while they searched him, his hands on the roof of the car.

In one of the photos, he's climbing a tree, supported in the arms of a fork. A yellow baseball cap throws a shadow over his forehead. He's looking at the camera from above with a startled expression, as if he'd been caught by surprise. A boy climbing a tree. There should be joy, but it's absent. It's not the image of a child at play, but of someone looking for shelter in the canopy.

In another photo he's squinting, as if the light were blinding him. His expression suggests worry and a degree of maturity beyond his years. It was taken in a park. There are trees in the background. Though he posed for the photo, he didn't want his picture taken – and it shows. Even so, it's a lovely closeup, his face clean, handsome. This photo marks the definitive end of his childhood.

I also want to talk about a group photo in which he and his mother are standing next to some relatives of hers. There's an uncle and his wife, both born in Poland, and their teenage daughter, born in Brazil – all with pale, Slavic complexions. They wear forced smiles. He looks serious and ostentatiously indifferent, his hands in his jacket pockets. His mother looks uncomfortable. What most stands out in this photo is the difference in physical types. His condition as adopted child is already an integral part of his personality, his public image, his place in the world. He is nine, or a little older, and he knows that genealogy isn't his: that he is an offshoot from some other trunk, the roots of which he is ignorant.

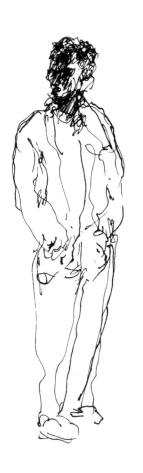

18.

The name is terrifying. *Dead mother complex.* Had we known about it at the time, we wouldn't have left him in Michigan, living in someone else's house, going to school with strangers, in a strange country with a strange language. We had spent a year in Lansing, the state capital, where we had a close friend. My wife was on a sabbatical year; I took a screenwriting course. When it was time to come home, he wanted to stay. He was at that age when friends are the most important thing, and during the year we spent there he had made plenty of them.

Without giving it too much thought, we agreed. We thought it would be good for him to continue studying at an American school, with decent teaching and the chance to consolidate his English. Perhaps it had already occurred to me that in a racist world, he would need some extra tools to survive. A black kid who has studied in the United States and speaks English isn't just any black kid.

Our friend in Michigan, who was the mother of his best friend and classmate, generously offered to host him. We had total confidence in her. She had lived in Brazil during the worst years of the dictatorship and had been my partner in a documentary about the Trans-Amazonian Highway. We negotiated the conditions of his stay there, and he became a weekly boarder at the same school. We came back to Brazil, and he stayed. The idea was that he would finish junior high. It was another two years.

Dead mother complex isn't a clinical condition. It's a theoretical construction by the French psychoanalyst André Green, who studied situations in which the child suddenly loses the affection of its mother without having anything to replace it with, like when she falls into depression. She is present, but in the child's imagination it's as if she had died. In Green's terminology, the child suffers a psychic catastrophe. Some of these children will end up psychotic or schizophrenic, as the American psychiatrist Bruce Perry argues in his impressive report on traumatized children, *The Boy who was Raised as a Dog.*

If the separation is brief, the child can reconstruct its emotional world. But if it's long, the child's sense of its own omnipotence unravels, and they lose confidence in themselves and in the world. The feeling of abandonment will accompany such children for the rest of their life, merging with their personality and becoming manifest in the form of phobias.

It really doesn't take much for a child to feel abandoned or unloved. And we left him there, far from us – an adopted son who had already been abandoned by his biological mother and was conscious of that. He was at that tricky, delicate phase after the onset of puberty, at the beginning of adolescence. This is a time when children are torn by contradictory impulses, sometimes dangerously isolating themselves from the real world. Having read the English psychoanalyst Donald Winnicott, I now know that adopted children are even more demanding and sensitive than biological children; they should never be abandoned, not even in adolescence.

At the end of his first year without us, he became depressed. Winter in Michigan is cold and wet. The nights are long, the rain heavy. Even in summer, the landscape is desolate. People travel long distances by car from one shopping centre to another. It's a vast expanse of soy, corn, and beet fields. He got the flu, followed by bronchitis. Back then we blamed his depression on the flu. Today, I think it was dead mother complex. He was fourteen.

19.

It's gone midnight, and he still hasn't got in. He went out to surf and hasn't come back. I'm tormented by a series of wild hypotheses, all of which feature the groundsman next door. He's a very dark-skinned man with a drunkard's bloodshot eyes. It was obvious he hated the boy. You could tell from his threatening gestures. He'd been trimming the hedge with angry blows of his machete, as if he were chopping off heads. And from his rough way of dumping the branches in that enormous cart, casting sideways glances in our direction. In the boy's direction.

I go out looking for him in the car, accelerating recklessly. Once I get to the main road I realise that I might come across him on his way back and I slow down. In a low gear, I peer carefully at the roadside. The shops are closed. The night is dark, overcast. I stop at the entrance to each of the little streets that lead down to the sea and squint between the houses. There are no lights on, no living soul.

To my surprise, there's a single bar which is still open. Hopeful, I park the car. I ask the owner, who's mopping the floor, if he has seen a boy matching his description. "No, he hasn't been here." Further on there's a petrol station all lit up like something from a fairy tale, but there's nobody there. A car overtakes me as I'm driving up Morro da Neblina; the driver glances at me as he passes, curious as to why I'm going so slowly. At the top of the hill, my gaze takes in the distant semicircle of lights around the little bay and I wonder which beach he's on. Or which bar he's in. Which filthy hole. The sea is a dark stain. Sinister. I feel the first rumbles of panic.

On the other side of the hill, the road runs alongside Praia Mole for a couple of kilometres. It's not a surfing beach; it has a steep shelf and fearsome waves that can drag you down. He can't be there. Even so, I drive slowly, looking at every bench, the trunk of every palm tree. I think again about the groundsman, his strange behaviour. He's a muscular black guy, always shirtless, with reddish eyes. Lurid headlines flash across my mind: "Child sacrificed in voodoo ritual".

What did we ever do to him? Our boy has done him no harm. He must be jealous, bitterly jealous. Maybe he's lost a son of the same age. Or maybe he can't accept the good life the boy has, as he has to look after a rich family's house and live in a little annex on the side. He's taken it out on the boy! I could feel the envy in the way he was glaring at him. My God! What if he's abducted him? I drive nervously, imagining the worst. That brute must have jumped the boy as soon as he opened the gate to leave. Then he killed him with a single blow from his machete, threw his body on the cart with the garden waste, and dumped the lot in a muddy trench somewhere amongst the rushes.

The next beach isn't a surfing beach either. I park the car anyway and comb it on foot, walking back and forth between the palm trees, hoping to find him lying on the sand somewhere. Nothing. Back in the car, I'm overcome once again by sinister thoughts. I can't get the image of the black guy with the machete out of my head. At the same time, I know it's ridiculous. I feel like I'm getting paranoid. I lean against the steering wheel and stay that way until I calm down.

I get back on the road, headlights at full beam. I crest another hill and reach the bay where the surfing beach begins. So many times I've given him a lift out here to surf. This time he came on the bus. I get out of the car at the start of the beach and walk in zigzags between the coconut palms and shuttered kiosks. My shoes sink into the sand, only increasing my sense of helplessness. Every ten steps I call his name.

I sit down on the sand to think. I need to act rationally. Panic achieves nothing. I look around. There's usually a lone shellfish-picker, or a fisherman standing knee-deep in the shallows. But tonight there's nobody. I head towards the hotel that occupies the central section of the bay. It's totally dark, closed. There's a sign saying that the reception will open at five. I check the time: half past three. But there's a bell, which I ring repeatedly. Finally a light comes on and an old man appears, rubbing his eyes. I ask if he has seen a boy – a boy like this. "No", he says, grumpily. "Are you sure?" I ask. "I've been here since seven," he says, "when my shift began." I ask if he's heard anything about a boy having drowned. "No, we would know if something like that had happened", he says. Then, in a kinder tone, "Why don't you try the bakery, on the other side of the road? They open at five, but by half four there are people there."

I go back to the car and drive to the other side of the bay. I get out and resume the search on foot. I peer into each alley between the houses, each gulley of the slope. Nothing. He had to be somewhere on that beach. But he wasn't. Panic returns. That brute must have done something to the boy. His way of pacing around, brandishing his machete. The son of a bitch.

Two more hours and it'll be dawn. Should I wait for day to come, or should I go back? Perhaps I'll catch the groundsman red handed? Or I could burst into his annex and beat the truth out of him! I turn the car around and head back, imagining the worst. I feel beside myself. Obsessed with the groundsman. He killed him. That dirty look, always following the boy. Or maybe the boy did something and hasn't told me. He shouldn't mix with people like that. I told him, "Be careful with the groundsman next door, he doesn't look right in the head". He didn't listen. He never listens. I drive frantically. I can't get the groundsman's machete out of my head. At the same time, I cling to the hope of finding the boy at home. He might have come back whilst I've been out. I find the annex dark and the cart parked in its usual place, still full of garden waste. I'm suddenly aware of how stupid my suspicions are. Inside the house my wife is sobbing. "He hasn't come back", she says.

I go out again. This time I drive the thirty kilometres out to the surfing beach without stopping. It's still dark when I arrive, but I can see a light on in the bakery. They're raising the shutters. I park out the front, ask for him, describe him the best I can. A boy like this: tall, slim, light brown skin, a white surfboard. "Yes, a boy like that asked me for some food on tick", the man says. "I wouldn't normally do it, but I felt sorry for him. I think he's over there, underneath an awning. Take a look behind that garage, there's always someone asleep there." I thank him and walk off hurriedly in the direction indicated.

And there he is, spread out on the ground, his head resting on his surfboard. I feel an enormous, indescribable sense of relief. The remains of his takeaway are at his side. First I kick it away, then I kick him. "Come on!" I yell. He gets up, walks towards the car, dragging his feet, dragging his board. "How much for the food?" I ask back at the bakery. I pay up and thank them. That was when he was fifteen.

A year later, he had to undergo the dreaded knee operation which Dr Andreucci had predicted back when he was small. His kneecaps couldn't take the stress of surfing.

20.

In Michigan, he took up piano and guitar. Once back in São Paulo, we proposed that he study at the Shakespeare, a school for the rich, for diplomats' kids, which had a strong reputation for art and music. To get a place, you needed a recommendation from another parent with a child already at the school, like at a private members' club. My friend Stephan, an American cameraman who had lived in São Paulo for years, duly obliged.

The headteacher was also called Stephan, a fat, cantankerous Irishman with a strict reputation. Hereafter he'll be Mr Stephan, to distinguish him from my friend. Only after Mr Stephan had subjected the boy to a rigorous interrogation was he allowed to enrol. But late one morning just three months later, Mr Stephan telephoned me. "Come and pick up your son immediately", he said. "He's expelled. He was caught with another two boys in possession of marijuana."

The school building is set back almost a hundred metres from the street, by a lawn. They wouldn't even let me through the outside gate. Expulsion is a degrading ritual. They lock the student in a little room, like in solitary confinement, until someone comes to get them. They are then escorted to

44

the gate, handed over, and ordered to never come back, as if parent and child had both become equally leprous.

He walked over slowly, his rucksack hanging off one shoulder. His expression was serious, but to me he also seemed somehow defiant, with perhaps even a trace of pride in his crime. I swung at his nose as soon as he was close enough. He put his left hand to a trickle of blood, but said nothing. I didn't do it because of the weed, though I was no fan of the stuff, but because of his stupidity, for having wasted the chance of a privileged education. But I regret throwing that punch today. And I wonder whether he would have done something so stupid if he could have smoked freely at home, as our friends' children did.

I decided to fight it, to turn my anger against Mr Stephan. It might be a foreign-run institution, but we were in Brazil and his expulsion contravened the statute of the child and the adolescent. What kind of education is this? Rather than attempting to tackle an adolescent's behavioural problem, it simply tosses them aside. It's a form of violence, and it's hypocritical to boot. But hypocrisy was everywhere. There was a school popular amongst our friends, run by sixties rebels like us, who had all smoked in their youth – and it too expelled any student caught with weed. Charlatans, the lot of them! They just wanted to sterilize their schools.

In the end, for reasons I can't recall, I decided not to fight the expulsion. Weakness? Lack of determination? Perhaps. Today I think that the expulsion from the Shakespeare was also his expulsion from paradise. It signalled the end of his adolescence and determined what was to come, starting with the pursuit, first hesitant but then obsessive, of an artificial paradise. And I blame myself for not waking up to that in time.

Some months later, Mr Stephan and his Victorian hypocrisy would become a case for the police.

21.

MYSTERIOUS CRIME SHOCKS SÃO PAULO ELITE

The headteacher of the renowned Shakespeare College, Mr Stephan O'Connor, was found dead yesterday in the neighbourhood of Jardins. He appeared to have been tortured and strangled. Inspector Paulo Mendes, of the Jardins district, told this report that the crime must have occurred on Saturday night. School employees became concerned when O'Connor did not appear for work on Monday and after the failure of repeated attempts to contact him by telephone. They went to look for him at his apartment, which was opened by the building's caretaker.

The headteacher's body was found naked, tied to a chair, and displaying signs of torture. Inspector Mendes believes it was an attempt at extortion, followed by homicide. The perpetrator was known to the victim, as there were no signs of a break in. José Gomes, the caretaker, said that for some time he had suspected that Mr O'Connor had been receiving visitors through the garage door in the early hours of the morning. Inspector Mendes believes the perpetrator is a male escort, and said in this type of case it is common for victims to ensure that nobody sees their visitor.

22.

The expression "artificial paradise" comes from Baudelaire. Since time immemorial, man has been searching for the formula that will return him to the delights of paradise, whether in aphrodisiacs, hallucinogens, or narcotics. Helen gives Telemachus a drink to soothe his pain, while Odysseus's sailors are seduced with lotus flowers. Opium and morphine were popular in Europe in Baudelaire's time, though in fact he was referring to hashish, the resin of *Cannabis sativa*. It came from Algeria, where it had replaced alcohol, forbidden under Islamic law. These days, we smoke dried and compressed *Cannabis sativa* leaves like tobacco – weed, in layman's terms, though it has an infinite array of names: *skunk, draw, green, gange, ganja, Mary Jane, dope, grass, herb, pot, puff, bud, bhang, sinsemilla, chronic, smoke, blow, reefer, hydro, leaf, shit, bush.* Almost as many names as the devil. And one more, in the words of the law forbidding its possession: *a psychoactive substance.*

Cannabis sativa is a hardy plant; it can grow in any soil. The hippies planted it in their gardens and lauded it as the sacramental potion of a new lifestyle, the authentic existence championed by Sartre and the counterculture. In similar fashion, Timothy Leary espoused the virtues of mescaline. In the novel they wrote together, William Burroughs and Jack Kerouac revealed that a stick of weed cost just ten cents. With the Second World War it went up to fifty – even so, a pittance.

During the most repressive years of the Brazilian dictatorship, the military condemned weed as a tool of international communism with which to destroy the traditional family and Christian values. But teenagers were just as desperate to try weed as they were to get laid. As their mothers were worried about them getting into trouble out on the street, they would beg them to invite their friends inside to smoke. Rolling a joint was normal amongst my filmmaker friends. To hide it, they would remove the tobacco from a normal cigarette and fill it with weed. Or they'd stuff it into the hole of the Kodak film rolls, which held enough weed for a few joints. One director smuggled three hundred kilos from Paraguay to finance a film. But they wouldn't even bother offering it to me. I was the "hip square" – happy around smokers, though I didn't indulge myself. Weed scared me. While for some it was Baudelaire's artificial paradise, for me it was the apple of original sin, which once I had tried it, would lead me onto who knows what. Today this type of usage is called "recreational", like going to the cinema or reading a detective novel. An inoffensive, pleasurable activity.

Baudelaire predicted that once man had entered the artificial paradise, he wouldn't be able to escape the fatality of his temperament. He called hashish the mirror that just amplifies whatever is already within the individual. I read – during these belated investigations of mine – that high doses of *Cannabis sativa* can provoke hallucinations and cause impotence. Those who start in adolescence – like he did – can suffer significant and irreversible impairment of their ability to reason, even if their usage is only recreational. The risk of becoming addicted is also greater. And once addiction is present, it will hold them hostage.

23.

It says in the enclosed report that the military police were on a routine patrol in the Serra do Itatiaia forest reserve when they approached the suspect, who was behaving suspiciously. A subsequent search found nothing on his person, though inside his vehicle they found what they believed to be a quantity of a psychoactive substance and a cigarette. The forensic analysis confirmed this, as shown in the enclosed document. Charges were brought, but as the maximum custodial sentence that may be imposed for this crime is a year, and as the accused is not facing any other charges, has not been convicted of any other crime, and fulfils the other requirements of Article 77 of the Penal Code, I declare valid the proposal by the public prosecutor of a two-year suspended sentence, during which the accused must abide by certain extra-penal rules of conduct, as follows: 1) he is forbidden to visit places of ill repute; 2) he is prohibited from leaving his county of residence for more than eight days without judicial authorization; 3) he must attend a quarterly court hearing to provide evidence of and justify his activities during this time. The accused must confirm his agreement with these conditions. Once the period of the sentence has passed without incident, the case will be closed. If the accused is found to be in breach of these conditions, the case will resume. Once read and found to be in order, this document will be registered.

24.

The Brazilian police are zealous about catching boys with weed. If the boys look rich, they'll threaten them with prison and demand a bribe. If they're black or brown or they look poor, they'll arrest them, to make it look like they're doing their duty and make up for letting the rich kids go free. They're not necessarily detained for long, but they're always processed and given a record. That's what happened to him. I remember that I asked a lawyer friend of mine to contest it and have the case annulled. He was a father of two teenagers, and had more experience in such matters than me. "Let me give you a piece of advice", he said. "Let it go, it'll serve as a deterrent." So that's what I did.

25.

Karl Neuman, better known as Carlinhos, had only just turned eighteen when he did the editing for my documentary on the Cabanagem rebellion. He did a fine job. The Cabanagem had piqued my interest because it was one of the first great rebellions of the Brazilian poor. And the first time they were massacred. Thirty thousand dead. When my Lebanese grandparents arrived in Manaus in 1910, there were only a few locals who could still remember it. The rebels were destitute Indians and *mestiços*, who lived in *cabanas*, houses on stilts on the banks of the Amazon. Forging an alliance with small-scale merchants and farmers, in 1835 they embarked on a desperate struggle for political independence. Ever since I first heard my grandfather pronounce the word *Cabanagem*, it had been magical to me, staying with me ever since. I was also drawn to the Cabanagem for practical reasons. The photographer André Penteado had published an album of portraits of the descendants of the rebels and the followers of the rebel leader, the canon Batista Campos, whose bones rest in the chapel in São Francisco Xavier, near Barcarena, in the state of Pará. With the research given to me on a plate and the locations and participants identified, filming was easy and cheap. At the event in New York, *The War of the River People* won the award for best editing. Back in Brazil, I wanted to share the good news with Carlinhos, but I was surprised to find his office closed. I rang his father, Leopold, a friend from way back and the owner of a large photography shop. They are a Hungarian Jewish family from a left-wing political tradition, all involved in photography. The name Karl was a tribute to Marx, while his sister Rosa was named after Rosa Luxemburg. "Carlinhos isn't well", his father told me. "What's wrong with him?" I asked. "Is it serious?" Leopold didn't answer. "Come by the shop and I'll explain", he said. So I went over and he revealed, in a murmur, that his son was a cocaine addict. "Every so often he'll relapse and lock himself in his room", he said. "He's not rowdy or violent, he just locks himself away for a week or two. This time it's worse: his girlfriend left him, and he's been locked in his room for almost the last month; he only comes out to use the bathroom. His mother takes him food." "Why didn't you say anything?" I asked. "If I had, would you have hired him? Would you have trusted him?" I had to admit not. "And he came up trumps, didn't he?" He did. "And you won that prize, didn't you?" There was a sudden change in Leopold's tone of voice, in which I could sense great pain. Without answering, I gave him a hug.

26.

A phone call. "I've left your son in the emergency room at the Hospital das Clínicas." "What happened?" I ask. "Who are you?" "You don't know me, I'm a friend of his." "But what happened?" I ask again, virtually yelling into the phone. "They said he's in an alcohol-induced coma; he won't speak or react." "When was this?" "Right now, I've just left him there." "And where did you get my number from?" "I had it from before; we hang out a lot."

He must have been sixteen or seventeen. I later found out that this was not the first time. He and his friends would sit and drink at plastic tables outside bars on street corners; the wind from both directions was ideal for clearing the unmistakeable stench of weed. First they would drink, then pass round joints. Alcohol is a depressant; *Cannabis sativa* a stimulant. It was like crouching, before springing into the great leap towards the artificial paradise.

Drinking too much, too fast, can lead to alcoholic coma, which in turn can cause heart failure. It happens to teenagers who have yet to work out how their bodies react to alcohol. The liver takes an hour to process a can of beer, a glass of wine, or a measure of spirits. When more than five drinks are consumed at once, there is a risk of coma. With ten, there's danger of death.

At that bar, they drank beer. The ancients got drunk on wine. They believed it was a gift from the gods, providing a metaphysical sensation of bliss and harmony and keeping at bay the feelings of fear and weariness inherent to their hard lives. Beer has always existed, first as a source of nourishment, then, with the growth of towns around the cultivation of cereals, as the intoxicant of the common man. It may be weaker than wine, but it's just as dangerous.

William James gives alcohol a central role in human history, for its ability to stimulate our mystical faculties. "Sobriety diminishes, discriminates, and says no; drunkenness expands, unites, and says yes." That's why we celebrate wine. "A full goblet of wine at the right time is worth more than all the kingdoms of this earth", Mahler would proclaim in *The Song of the Earth*. "Now, drink the wine! Now is the time, comrades! Drain your golden goblets to the last!"

Years after that phone call, which I confess I gave little importance at the time, alcohol would be the trigger for his every relapse. A single drink was enough to set him on the path towards chaos.

27.

We used to travel. Short trips and longer journeys. The Pantanal in Mato Grosso, the Epitácio hot springs, Iguazu Falls, the caverns of Paraná, the Chapada dos Veadeiros National Park. With every trip came new feelings about the world, new adventures, new discoveries. He loved it; he was fascinated. His eyes would shine, ecstatic.

The trip to Patagonia was our last, and the most stunning of all. We flew to Ushuaia, via Santiago de Chile, where we visited the notorious penal colony, now a museum, where dozens of Argentine anarchists were locked up, including their famous leader, Simón Radowitsky. He was impressed by the inscriptions preserved in some of the cells; we read them carefully. The town of Ushuaia grew up around that prison.

After that, we made the extraordinary crossing of the Beagle Strait, the boat passing vast ice fields of a dazzling white. It was otherworldly, different from anything we had seen. In the photos he's tall and good-looking. He's seventeen. His face is handsome, his complexion clear. His hair is a mass of tight black curls, his eyes just as dark. His eyebrows are thick, and he wears a wispy moustache. In most of the photos his posture is rigid and his gaze distant. He seems troubled. Something is bothering him. He was like that for the whole trip. He wasn't an adult, but he wasn't a kid any more either. Life was no longer a dream, and holidaying with his parents had become more of a punishment than an adventure. The cheerful, gracious boy he had been, full of *joie de vivre*, had become a distant young man with a sombre look.

In one of the photos we have our arms around each other, wearing the yellow lifejackets they made us wear while trekking on the formidable glaciers. In that photo of a hug between father and son I see a paradoxical combination of affection and awkwardness: affection from my side, awkwardness from his. It was a hug which could do nothing to erase the distance between his thoughts and mine.

28.

My generation, the children and grandchildren of immigrants, received a basic and sometimes crude upbringing. Many of our parents saw beating their children as the way to educate them. And children didn't have their own personality; they were just blank slates for their parents to write on. As if to make amends for this, my generation put the child on a pedestal, like a little god. With this came therapy, from an early age. Difficulties making friends at preschool? Play therapy, Melanie Klein. Bad marks in primary school? Attention deficit disorder, Kumon, and sessions with the developmental psychologist. Depression in adolescence? Psychotherapy.

Once he had definitively gone off the rails, we resorted to heavy psycho-analysis. Freud. Three sessions a week. They all told us it was vital, though it wouldn't be enough. This taught us a new lesson: an initiation in psycho-analysts who were ill-prepared, foolish, or remiss. There was one young psychoanalyst who was very serious and extremely expensive. By chance, we discovered that he hadn't been turning up to his sessions. When we questioned her, she claimed that notifying us would have constituted a breach of client–therapist confidentiality. He hadn't been for a whole month. She had scarcely managed to establish a bond with him, and yet she had the nerve to talk about violating confidentiality.

Then there are the jaded ones, who, after a lifetime of disappointment, have stopped believing in their own medicine and resort to easy solutions for themselves and the families they're supposed to be helping. So many opt for mediocrity in this way. One of them, drunk on the police-like power that society grants doctors, suggested getting him sectioned as a psychotic. He had a whole team of goons at his disposal, ready to restrain him. But I knew my Foucault and recognised this as medicine as social control. I told the doctor to get fucked.

We had exhausted all other options when I discovered a special treatment, a week-long intensive course at a hotel out in the countryside. It was expensive. Really expensive. At the end of the course, there was a ceremony at the headquarters of the institution, where each participant gave a short, emotional speech in which they declared themselves free of all their demons. The audience – consisting almost exclusively of wealthy families – rejoiced. It was an aggressive exercise in self-deception. A few days later, he relapsed. I no longer remember the name of that particular method. I do know a general term though. It's called charlatanism.

There's an expression I've never forgotten which came out of all that. I was particularly intrigued by his lack of principles and feelings of guilt. He showed no signs of shame or remorse; it was as if he had no superego, or simply that nothing mattered to him any more. I know people tend to think and act in ways which make life easier. But … he was such an able, intelligent young man! With his whole life ahead of him! I asked my therapist – not his – if drug addiction had corroded his character, or whether it was the other way around – that this lack of character was there to begin with and it was that which had led him to addiction. The therapist's first response was philosophical. "An adult without principles is also an adult without character," he said, "because if he had acquired any character he would feel the need for principles." Then he gave me the clinical diagnosis: "personality disorder". That was all he said.

What type of disorder? And to what degree? Severe? Moderate? Reversible? Incurable? We needed to go beyond generic terminology. We consulted a reputed Argentine psychiatrist, who had been recommended to us by friends. He listened to us with great interest. He wanted to know more and more. He charged us for every minute of it and didn't explain a thing.

The American psychologist Dan Kiley coined the expression Peter Pan syndrome to refer to adults who behave like eternal children. The natural selfishness of childhood means that they always want to receive, never to give; they shirk their responsibilities. This was typical of his relationships with women. He had no trouble getting girlfriends, but he would leave them as soon as they mentioned marriage, children, or even just moving in together. Or, having been separated from his biological mother, was he just breaking the bonds before they became too tight, fearing separation further down the line? It's possible.

29.

Other parents would talk about their children – and we kept quiet. They would talk of how clever they were – and we kept quiet. Of how hardworking they were – and we kept quiet. Of how talented they were – and we kept quiet. We kept quiet, we kept quiet, we kept quiet. We kept quiet for a long time. Why stigmatize him? Nobody needed to know. It would pass.

Until one day, though still hesitant, we let a word slip to one of our closest friends. A word no more; just discreetly letting off some steam. "He's not very well. There's a problem." Then the friend opened up. They too had been keeping quiet. This discovery comforted us. It shouldn't have, but it did. We may not have liked to admit it, but it did. It was as if their sorrows relieved our own. Quietly, we listened to their story, and quietly they listened to ours. We exchanged addresses, pieces of advice. Afterwards, we said no more about our children.

30.

I went into the study and found him smoking through a hole in a crushed beer can and watching porn on the computer. Totally out of it. You were filming the Palestinians down south; I didn't know which town you were in and even if I had, I wasn't going to interrupt your work. Fortunately, Ferreira helped me out. First, he pulled him out of the chair and dragged him from the study. I thought he wouldn't be able to, but he didn't resist. I locked him in the storeroom. There was no doubt in my mind at all, we had to get him into rehab as planned. Just as well you had left me the address and the phone number of the clinic that Márcio had recommended. But I needed someone to stay by his side while I drove the car, preferably a man. Jairo was on a viva examination committee. Élvio couldn't do it either. But there was Ferreira. "Give me half an hour to cancel some things", he said. Only then did I let him out of the storeroom, telling him to pack for rehab. He didn't say anything, not a word, just obeying like a little dog. He shoved some clothes and a toothbrush inside a backpack and sat down on the edge of the bed, waiting. I didn't need to ask whether he agreed with it or not. I waited for Ferreira, relieved at having taken the decision to put him into rehab. Ferreira arrived and the three of us set off for Campinas, him slumped in the back seat with his backpack alongside him. We followed the directions they had given me on the phone, coming off the Bandeirantes Highway at kilometre 95 and taking a service road. We passed a cemetery and a landfill site, until we arrived at the address they had given me. It was a desolate spot. The clinic was the only building on the street and it was surrounded by a three-metre high wall. The plot it occupied was small, maybe just fifty by fifty metres. At the main gate there was a guardhouse, with a discreet sign displaying the name of the clinic: Caminho da Paz. The admissions procedure was brief; the attendant filled in a form, asking few questions, as if they already knew everything. He remained passive. Then they showed us around. There were three buildings, two of which were obviously quite old. In the biggest one there was a common room; the accommodation was in the other. A smaller building with a covered patio served as a kitchen and dining room. Márcio had warned me beforehand that it was a poor, run-down clinic, but even so, I didn't like what I saw. There was a little garden with some benches and a well in the centre, covered with wooden boards. There were just a few people sitting around: some of them young; some older, with a grim appearance. They had this funny look in their eyes, as if they were trying to hide their sense of defeat with a false show of confidence and happiness. It was useless. It was an ugly, wretched place. That was when the penny dropped. He had just entered the first circle of hell. And us with him. I think he knew that as soon as I mentioned rehab. They know. They talk to each other. We're the ones who have no idea. As we were leaving we ran into the founder of the clinic, a recovering alcoholic. He talked of the place with bitterness. Most patients leave supposedly cured only to return a few weeks later. Almost all of the older residents were alcoholics, while almost all of the younger ones were crack addicts.

31.

He was barely an adolescent when crack appeared in Brazil. Five times stronger than cocaine and ten times cheaper, crack is the drug of choice of the poor, the homeless and the prison population. And adolescents. It is smoked in homemade pipes using metal tubes. He must have only been starting out because he didn't have the tube; he had improvised using a beer can. The intense euphoria produced by crack has been described like a lightning bolt, the "buzz" as it's known in the drug slang. But what follows this buzz, which doesn't last for long, is a feeling so awful that you have to have another hit. And another, and another. The only other addiction it can be compared to is heroin. In his autobiographical novel *Junkie*, William Burroughs describes the constant, frantic search for heroin in the backstreets of New York, New Orleans, and Mexico City. With no will of his own, Burroughs was living only to score and keep away the sickness, as they say. Likewise, a crack addict will do anything for a hit. They will abandon their work, their studies, or any interest other than the insatiable search for the rock.

They will sell anything of value in the house. They will steal from their parents and grandparents. If they have a girlfriend, they will beat her money out of her. Over the years that followed, he did all of this. That's what led me to write the letter.

32.

They say we remember whatever has been significant for us. I've always had a lousy memory, but I still remember the teachers, the other participants, and the room in the back of that gallery. I even remember the restaurant where we had lunch in the interval between the two sessions. It was an all-day conference, on a Sunday, for the parents of addicts. It was Leopold who told me about it, though he didn't attend. Three hundred *reais* a head. My wife didn't want to go either; she thought it was pointless. She was always quicker than me to grasp what was going on. I was still deceiving myself.

I found myself amongst a dozen other parents. Simple people. Housewives, low-level civil servants. Frightened people who no longer cared about exposing themselves. Being there was a decisive step. I admitted being the father of an addict. A co-dependent, in the clinical jargon. I was taking publicly the step that my wife had already taken in private. I think I was the only one there from an intellectual background.

The workshops were given by a psychologist, a retired police chief, and a lawyer. They didn't mince their words. They wanted to give us a jolt, and that's exactly what they did. Theirs was a firm criminal and moralistic stance, without psychological nuances or indulgent excuses. They emphasized the extraordinary gravity of dependence on psychoactive substances and the near impossibility of breaking it. It was a gloomy prognosis. They told us to look after ourselves, because the struggle that lay ahead of us would be a long one, and it almost always ended in defeat.

Everything they predicted in that workshop would come true, though I knew nothing of such things at the time. It was my first formal lesson on the subject, and it had a profound effect on me. At the end, they showed the film *The Basketball Diaries*, in which Leonardo DiCaprio plays a boy who gets into cocaine at just thirteen. It must have been his first film. I've always liked it, not just for DiCaprio's exceptional performance, but for the moral of the story, the way it outlines every step of the descent into hell. The first innocent lines he does with friends, feeling invincible, kings of the world. The lack of dialogue with his mother, the hypocrisy of his father. The impotence of a school paralyzed by bureaucracy. His first loss, a friend who dies of leukaemia. The first time he shoots up; the first time he's expelled; the first time he steals; the first time he's arrested; then the street and ultimately prostitution, the final circle of hell.

33.

Our film *Tropical Palestine*, about the Palestinian diaspora, wasn't as successful as *The War of the River People*. It was criticised by Palestinian leaders for not emphasizing the concept of the Palestinian nation and by leaders of the Jewish community for dramatizing the suffering of thousands of Palestinian families who live in refugee camps to this day.

Still, the sense of exile that Abou had spoken of – the feeling of being far from crops and communities, rather than from a country or nation state – did come across in the interviews. It's a unique concept of diaspora: the scattering of the extended family, the clan, defined by the paternal line. This is the cause of far greater resentment than simply being far from a motherland.

I did a lot of filming on the border with Uruguay, home to half of the nearly 100,000 Palestinians who emigrated to Brazil, most of them during the 1940s. As I worked, I would send the films to Abou, who would then find the remaining members of those families in Israel and the territories controlled by the Palestinian National Authority. Abou came over for the editing, which was done by Carlinhos. Though he only stayed with us for a week, we managed to take him to the Serra da Mantiqueira, which blew him away.

34.

Suddenly, he would disappear. He would leave late in the afternoon, or at nightfall, and not come back. I'd be hanging on the telephone, expecting the worst. Then there were times he would leave for a fixed destination and fail to arrive. That's what happened with the intensive treatment at a hotel out in the countryside two hours from São Paulo. He left early but didn't show up. I rang them every hour, and the answer was always the same: your son still hasn't arrived. Then he rang me saying that he had got there. It was early in the morning. I could sense something untoward in his voice, and so I called the hotel. Your son still hasn't arrived, they said again. He didn't register until early the next morning, having missed the first day of treatment. I never found out what happened, and I didn't bother asking. Perhaps he spent the night in a roadside hotel with a prostitute he picked up along the way. His disappearances became frequent, as if a powerful force were compelling him to search places known only to him. Sometime later, in Belo Horizonte, where we had moved for a year as visiting professors at the Federal University of Minas Gerais, he would go out as soon as dusk fell.

I'd do nothing at first, but then I would start to panic and end up going out to look for him in the car. I would drive down the avenues around the park, then Avenida Amazonas, Avenida Afonso Pena, trying to make out his silhouette amongst the few pedestrians. He would sneak back in the small hours, just as quietly as he had gone out.

35.

We didn't know what to do with him after rehab. It wouldn't have been wise for him to return to where it all began. The newsboy he used to score from was still on the street, selling papers and dealing on the side. In our neighbourhood, he knew all the places you could pick up, and he knew all the other users. In a newspaper article, the renowned doctor Dráuzio Varella explained that drug cravings resurface as soon as one perceives the environmental and psychological stimuli connected to previous use of the substance. It's a conditioned reflex, of the type studied by Pavlov.

As he was going to resume his degree in music, we suggested he live close to the university, in Bela Vista. Provided he was studying, we'd pay his fees, plus two meals a day and rent for a room at a residence which we paid for directly, rather than put money into his hands. He was not to come to our neighbourhood. It was an urban exile. And a monetary penalty.

He went along with it because he had no alternative. As soon as he found a residence, I went to a bakery nearby and arranged to pay weekly for his breakfast and lunch. He did attend university, albeit sporadically.

It was a good course, but he still bunked off a lot. Occasionally he earnt a bit of extra cash helping out a painter and decorator. But he lived in poverty. I imagined him wandering the filthy streets of Bela Vista, my son, virtually a beggar. It hurt. Back then, it still hurt.

One afternoon, as I was paying the bill at the bakery, the owner revealed that he had been exchanging his lunch for beer. We hadn't bargained for this trick. This was another lesson. The specialists are wrong. It's no use just changing scenery. The scenery is the urge within them, and they carry it wherever they go. Whenever they arrive somewhere new, they work out where to pick up; they find others like them. I suppose they recognise each other by the searching gaze and the edgy walk; they've no need even for speech.

So nothing was resolved. Soon enough, he told us that he couldn't stay in the residence in Bela Vista. He told us that the guy he was sharing a room with was a crook and that the neighbourhood was crawling with dealers. He insisted on leaving immediately. I assumed he had run up a debt and was scared. Dealers have no mercy, and he never was much of a tough guy.

So we still had no idea what to do with him.

36.

— *Did you talk about your stepmother?*

— *Yes.*

— *How she used to punish you, how you went hungry?*

— *Yes, I told him everything.*

— *And how did he react?*

— *He was really surprised. He asked me a lot of questions; he wanted to know what had happened to my mum, and I told him nearly everything. I told him that my mum was only fifteen when she had me and that she handed me over to my dad before I turned three because she had no way of bringing me up. He listened to me very carefully, then he said that he felt very angry for having been abandoned.*

— *He used the word "abandoned"?*

— *Yes. He said that real mothers don't abandon their kids.*

— *And what did you say?*

— *What could I say? I explained that a mother doesn't abandon her child without good reason. If she does, then it's out of love, for the good of the* child. Then I had to see a client and we had to stop our conversation, but he waited and we carried on as soon as the appointment was over.

— Did you tell him about your work as a medium?

— Yes, he was interested. He said he was a medium as well and that he was an indigo child.

— What's an indigo child?

— Don't you know? They're special children who have come here to make the world a better place; they're gifted and can predict the future.

— How strange … where does that come from?

— From a book that was a famous a long time ago; not many people remember it today. It was written by a women who could see people's magnetic fields, their auras. Sometimes they were yellow, sometimes red, and then one day there appeared a boy with an indigo-coloured aura. She was a medium too.

— What a silly story.

— Well you would say that.

— What else did you tell him?

— I said that everything depends on the individual, not on their mother or father, nor on the doctors, nor anyone else.

— And what did he say?

— Nothing. He got up and left. I think he wants to hurt himself. He doesn't want to get out of the state he's in.

37.

I need to talk about his spiritism. He had a friend who was a medium; she got him into it. I wasn't interested in spiritism, but I was very fond of her and I trusted her judgement. I also knew of the Spiritist Federation's efforts to help addicts, and I figured that any kind of spiritual assistance was welcome. For the Italian psychoanalyst Luigi Zoja, there is a parallel between modern drug use and the rites of passage of ancient cultures. Perhaps spiritist ritual could have been a different rite of passage? Better late than never.

Zoja also argues that being born physically is insufficient; we also need to be born spiritually, which is achieved by assimilating symbols, cultural heritage, and initiation rites. But as we were from such different backgrounds – my roots in Maronite Lebanon, my wife's in the poverty-stricken Jewish villages of Eastern Europe – what kind of shared heritage could we have provided him?

An anthropologist friend of my wife gave him spiritist books of automatic writing and *The Gospel According to Spiritism* by Allan Kardec. This was how I found out that people from scientific backgrounds also believe in life after death, the transmigration of the soul, and reincarnation. Perplexed, I decided to do some research. For the psychologists, it's a case of narcissism. Narcissists are so much in love with themselves that they can't accept that the world will continue to exist without them. So they cling to the belief in an immortal soul. But I don't think that was the case with him. If he had truly been in love with himself, he wouldn't have been destroying himself with drugs. I concluded that his spiritism was an attempt to flee from the only certainty that we have: the here and now. Unable to face that, he took refuge in the hope of a second chance in a future life.

I also did some research on that indigo children nonsense. The woman who invented the concept is called Nancy Tappe; it became a New Age religion with thousands of converts in the United States. For the religious historian Sarah Whedon, the indigo child was a socially constructed response of American society to a crisis of childhood characterized by increasing violence and the proliferation of ADHD diagnosis.

I realised that in a short space of time, he had begun to read spiritist books exclusively. There was no space in his mind for the acquisition of other types of knowledge, like science. Spiritism also presents itself as a code of moral behaviour. It endorses the Ten Commandments handed down to Moses, an episode which Kardec interprets as a mediumistic communication between Moses and God. He claims that in each incarnation we have the opportunity to correct mistakes committed in previous ones, perfecting ourselves morally until we become a superior spirit. I began to wonder whether he was trying to communicate with the spirit of his biological mother. He certainly wasn't looking for moral perfection.

38.

It was the stamp that led to the idea of emigrating.

It was supposed to be his first on-the-books job. I remember it as if it were today, him coming back from the interview, ecstatic, with the news that he had been hired as a translator by the magazines *Billboard* and *Spin*, which were launching Brazilian editions. His studies in the United States had been worth it, I thought. That day he was wearing a white shirt, with well-ironed navy blue trousers. He looked elegant, fresh faced. He was in one of his rare clean phases. I imagined how happy he must have been, how much he must have dreamt of something like that.

The next day he came back early, looking dejected. He said that when he turned up for work, they made up an excuse and stamped CANCELLED where it said he had been hired on his employment record. We figured that they must have discovered his record for possession; his life was doomed before it had barely even started. What a disappointment. And with that black mark on his record, what was the point of sending applications to other companies? I realised that a storm was brewing and suggested that he migrated to a faraway Brazilian state, or maybe Canada or Australia, two English-speaking countries that had their doors open to immigrants.

Or even that he went to that most improbable of countries: Israel. Carlinhos was heading out as he had relatives there, and was hoping to work with Abou al-Walid, with whom he had become friendly during the editing of *Tropical Palestine*. As I was seeing him off, old Leopold took me aside and told me that the Israeli system for treating addicts was the best in the world. That must have been what swung it for me. I asked if anyone could go. "They have to prove that they have a Jewish mother or father", he responded, "Nationality doesn't matter; blood is what counts. It's the same rule in Italy for descendants of Italians and in Poland for descendants of Poles." "And how do you prove Jewish blood?" "From the family history and the surname, plus a testimony from a rabbi who's willing to vouch for him. They'll pay his fares and they'll give him a course in Hebrew once he gets there. But he's got to have the letter from the rabbi."

39.

He liked the idea. He had only just turned 25, and a journey into the unknown at that age is always tempting. Freedom, escape, adventure, renewal. But that didn't mean it wasn't also a banishment. It was as if subconsciously I wanted to free myself of him. I had banished him a long time before I sent the letter.

The day before he was due to travel he seemed very ill at ease. We threw a goodbye party, and friends and neighbours came. While they were mingling in the garden he went down to the garage, where one of the guests had left a motorbike. He went joyriding round the neighbourhood and crashed. He could have died. He travelled to Israel the next day with wounds on his knees and shoulders. I was worried they wouldn't let him board the plane.

There was a stopover in Zurich. A ten-hour wait. The small group he was with were going to take the opportunity to see the city and Lake Zurich. He was so agitated when he set off, and I was so paranoid, that I imagined the worst: he was going to get separated from the group, do something stupid, and miss the connection. I only calmed down when I spoke with Abou al-Walid on the phone and he told me that he had landed with the group in Israel, and was in an immigrant processing centre in a city called Ashkelon.

40.

When they're kids, our children lie to protect themselves from our anger; when they grow up, they lie to protect us from their failures. Human lies, which we pretend to believe in. But he lied to swindle us. Two days before he left for Israel I gave him a wristwatch. In the airport he wasn't wearing it. "Where's the watch?" I asked. "I was robbed outside a bar", he said. At the time I was sceptical, but I pretended to believe. I let it go. Today I ask myself why. Perhaps because I didn't want to know the truth. I took refuge in the doubt: who knows, perhaps he really was robbed? I had become a true co-dependent.

He hadn't been in Israel long before he asked for money. He said it was for a second-hand car. I suggested that he ask Abou al-Walid for advice. A few days later he said that Abou had seen the car and given his approval. I sent him the money, but instead of buying a car he bought a motorbike, knowing I wouldn't have given him the money for that. He lied about Abou and he lied about the car. He became a pizza delivery boy. Drug addicts like motorbikes; they make it easy to arrive at the most hidden places, cash in hand.

When I went to visit him, I found the motorbike left to rot at the back of a yard, missing various parts. I asked why he hadn't replied to my most recent emails. "My computer broke", he said. It was a laptop I had given him before he left. "Broke how?" I asked. "There was a short circuit on the network, and it overloaded the computer." "The short circuit made it all the way to the computer?" I asked. "Yes, that's right." "Have you tried to get any compensation from the electricity company?" I was suspicious. Lies tend to follow simple logic, and it would have been simpler just to repeat the explanation for the disappearance of the watch: I was robbed. Sometime later I would find the explanation in Dostoyevsky's *The Idiot*: to be believable, a lie has to be bigger than the one that came before it.

He didn't stop asking for money, inventing one need or another. And he never claimed compensation from the electricity company.

41.

The phone rings in the middle of the night. I look at the clock and calculate that in Israel day must have broken already. What can it be this time?

It's not him; it's a friend.

"Your son tried to kill himself."

"What!?"

"He drank washing-up liquid and some other cleaning products, but he's alright now."

"Where is he?"

"In the emergency room; he should be discharged today or tomorrow."

Two days later, I arrived in Israel. I felt troubled by gloomy thoughts throughout the journey. Suicide is so dramatic. It's unnatural, an affront to our most basic instinct: survival. Young men don't kill themselves on a whim or just because they've lost their self-esteem. Even less so in his case, given how much will to live he always had. You have to be suffering to the point of mental breakdown, feel that there is no way out, or that something dreadful is about to happen. It's not death that people desire exactly; rather, they want to put an end to their suffering.

I wondered whether that self-destructive impulse had been within him from childhood – without us knowing about it, without even him knowing about it – within that inaccessible other I that Winnicott calls the "true self". If that was the case, then no doubt he would keep trying until he was successful. I was distraught for the length of the 14-hour journey.

Abou al-Walid, whom I had told about my sudden trip, was waiting for me with his car at the airport. We hadn't seen each other since the screening of our film *Tropical Palestine* at the Berlin Film Festival five years previously. He seemed to have aged in that time. He received me with a hug, and I showed him the address they had given me in Tel Aviv. "It only takes 40 minutes from the airport into town", Abou said. His support was touching.

On the way he told me that Carlinhos had been doing well in Israel and was working for a television channel. They did the odd piece of freelance work together. I realised that Abou knew nothing about Carlinhos's drug problem, and so I said nothing. The address in Tel Aviv was for a kitchenette in the back of a tailor's. It was tiny, and there were mattresses everywhere.

I discovered that the so-called suicide was nothing of the sort. He had drunk a mixture of washing-up liquids that wouldn't have killed a cockroach. I couldn't help but think of Fernando Pessoa. "If you want to kill yourself, why don't you want to kill yourself?" At the time I interpreted the episode as a cry for help, but today I wouldn't even go that far. Perhaps he resorted to washing-up liquid because there was no other narcotic or stimulant to hand. In the desperate pursuit of the artificial paradise, some even drink battery acid.

42.

I've spoken of the lies, but not of the thefts. There was no shortage of warnings. I remember when I realised my Walkman – a device popular back in the 1990s – had gone missing. I was puzzled, but it never occurred to me that he had stolen it. In hindsight, that seems the only possible explanation. He was fifteen or sixteen. He didn't steal it so he could listen to music. He was like a child stealing a toy not to play with, but to get his mother's attention. Except in this case, his mother – perhaps his stepmother – was a psychoactive substance.

I'll never know what else he stole, though I know that he didn't stop. He went from stealing from his family to stealing from his friends. In Tel Aviv, he stole from the only friend who stuck with him, who had taken him in at the worst times. Ashamed of a crime I hadn't committed, I compensated the friend. A mistake. Co-dependence affects one's judgement. Then there was the disgraceful episode in which he stole his girlfriend's wages. As soon as she got back from work, he forced her to hand over her money. She was a sensitive girl, with a father absent since she was small, a sick mother, and a predatory brother. She was his girlfriend, and she loved him.

And he leeched off her. She was reluctant to go to the police, deceiving herself that he had only done it because he was off his head. He wasn't the one who had snatched the money from her hands; it was someone else, someone mad, someone possessed, like in a horror film. But what difference does it make? He is both his body and his mind. The madness is not external to him.

He got six months in jail for this incident. He was released having learnt nothing and without having changed in the slightest, promptly stealing a rucksack from the people who had been kind enough to take him in because they saw he had nowhere else to go. As there were personal documents in the rucksack they had to notify the police, and he was re-arrested. Feeling sorry for him, they withdrew the complaint and even paid his bail. Another mistake. Everyone does it. Everyone. None of us know how to deal with an evil which is both body and character.

According to the Brazilian Civil Code, theft is the surreptitious taking of someone's property, while robbery involves the use of force or the threat of it. Sentencing is heavier for the latter, as the assumption is that the robber is armed and often kills or wounds whoever resists. I think this is mistaken, because to steal surreptitiously is also to deprive the victim of the knowledge of who the thief is. And if it happens within a family or between friends, it's also stealing from a personal relationship. It's more than a crime against property: it's a crime against the spirit that unites friends, parents and children, brothers and sisters, boyfriends and girlfriends.

43.

— *Let's start with the first accusation. Threats. She said that you threatened her.*

— *With what?*

— *With violence.*

— *She's lying. If she had felt threatened, she would have gone to social services.*

— *So you deny the accusation?*

— *Yes.*

— *She also accuses you of extortion, of demanding money.*

— *Another lie. I don't need her money.*

— *You deny the accusation?*

— *Yes.*

— *Let's move on to the third accusation. She said that you broke things in the flat.*

— *What?*

— *A glass and the draining board in the kitchen.*

— *She's lying. Go and take a look if you like; you won't find anything broken.*

— *She said that this was before, in a different flat.*

— *She's making it up. The cat knocked over the glass, and the draining board was already cracked.*

— *So you deny the accusation?*

— *Yes.*

— *Let's move on to the most serious accusation, that of physical aggression.*

— *What aggression?*

— *She says that you put your hands around her neck and choked her, that you nearly strangled her.*

— *How can she say that without any proof?*

— *She also said you beat her head against the wall several times.*

— *It's all lies. I wasn't even there.*

— *She said you were under the influence when you returned home, and that's why you don't remember anything.*

— *That's another of her lies. I've been clean since the start of the year. I remember everything; I wasn't even at the flat.*

— *You're sure that you weren't there?*

— *Absolutely.*

— *Where were you?*

— *I was at a party.*

— *Why do you think she reported you then?*

— *Out of jealousy. She was pissed off I had gone to the party.*

— *But the next-door neighbour says that he heard her scream and that he heard noises.*

— *What kind of noises?*

— *Of something banging against the wall.*

— *So what? Maybe she was hammering something into the wall.*

— *He also said that you pushed another neighbour who went to help her.*

— *All lies.*

— *Five neighbours all said the same thing. How do you explain that?*

— *What did they say?*

— *That they heard her crying for help.*

— *They wanted to protect her, because she's a woman.*

— *Protect her from what, if you weren't there?*

— *I don't know. I don't like them. I reported one of them to the police for attacking me.*

— *Senhor Cohen?*

— *That's the one. He threatened me with a knife, so I reported him.*

— *Senhor Cohen says that you're the one who did that to him.*

— *He's lying. I don't like their lifestyle.*

— *Or perhaps it's that they're not too fond of yours?*

— *What's that supposed to mean?*

— *Senhor Cohen says that you and she would often fight.*

— *He's lying.*

— *So you deny the accusation of physical aggression?*

— *Yes.*

— *Senhor Cohen also said that you tried to steal a bicycle belonging to another resident.*

— *If I tried to steal his bicycle, why didn't he report it?*

— *Senhor Cohen says that he didn't report it because he stopped you from stealing it.*

— *So I didn't steal anything.*

— *He also said that subsequently the bicycle disappeared and that he's sure you're responsible. He said he thought it best to avoid you after that.*

— *That's his problem.*

44.

When he was in Year Six, his class put together a newspaper which surprised everyone for its confidence and the quality of its writing. It dealt with vandalism at school, adolescent anxieties, and even politics. He was one of the editors and wrote the leader columns. He had talent; he wasn't some mediocrity. Around the same time, he began writing a diary, a habit which he's never given up. He started writing compulsively, pages and pages covered with tiny letters, as if written by a prisoner who had no paper to waste.

After he left, I found a dozen or so notebooks and bundles of loose papers from his diary. I scanned a few pages, looking for some insight. They were meticulous accounts of his exploits, romantic adventures, and psychedelic experiences. In the few pages I read, there was no sign of regret or remorse, nor even of any doubt about the life he was living. He didn't mention us at all; it was as if we didn't exist. Perhaps he imagined himself without any parents at all, a test-tube baby, because to recognise our existence would have been to admit he had been rejected by his biological parents.

There were passages which contained peaks of euphoria and visions of a glorious future, but without any plan whatsoever. I concluded that it had never occurred to him to change. He had naturalized the behaviour which, paradoxically, was denaturing his life. Perhaps he would change once he hit rock bottom. But just erasing his mother and father wasn't enough. I also realised that once his habit of writing compulsively began to wane, what he wrote was no longer persuasive – it was banal. I think of the erratic but inspired diaries of Cocteau, or the hard-hitting memoirs of De Quincey, William Burroughs, and Hans Fallada, all valuable on both a human and literary level. But the talent he displayed when he edited the school newspaper went to waste.

45.

You come through a turnstile into an annex. It's an awful place. Scuffed floor, discoloured walls, broken plastic chairs. There are two counters. At one I sign in and hand over my passport, which will be returned when I leave. I'm informed that at the other counter I must pay for two packets of cigarettes, the maximum permitted per prisoner, and leave a few behind to pay for soft drinks and toothpaste. Even prisoners who don't smoke ask for cigarettes. They use them as currency.

While I wait I observe the others. There's a man in a grey suit and striped tie. An old man with a long white beard, spectacles with thin frames, and the crocheted kippah worn by orthodox Jews clipped onto his hair. There's a middle-aged woman with beautiful dark eyes, her head covered by a hijab. A blonde girl, in a low-cut top and short skirt, her face hidden behind dark sunglasses. Two old ladies together, both tiny, with wrinkled faces. A young man in shorts and T-shirt.

I wonder what misfortune can have befallen them. A son who got drunk and ran over an old woman? An older brother who killed his younger sister after she fell in love with someone she shouldn't have? The blonde in dark glasses could be an immigrant from Russia or Georgia. The Russians drink a lot, lose their heads, and beat their wives. There's also Russian mafia, or so I've read in the newspapers. They commit some terrible crimes: trafficking women, kidnapping, extorsion. Maybe it's her pimp who's inside. And what about the Orthodox Jew? Has he come to see a son or grandson? Perhaps he's one of those fanatics who destroy olive trees belonging to Arab farmers.

On the walls there are signs in Arabic, Russian, and Hebrew. The Hebrew script is hard, with straight lines, as if carved with a chisel. The Arabic is flowing and graceful, delicately traced with a brush. The Russian Cyrillic uses what look like our Latin letters, but half of them face the wrong way. Three such different types of writing. I understand none of them.

While the signs say nothing to me, the visitors say nothing to each other. Each one carries their own burden. There's no solemnity at all, just sadness. The blonde girl is filing her nails. The Arab woman in the satin hijab remains lost in thought. This forced coexistence of strangers has been dragging on for an hour already.

Finally, we're directed to a patio, where a guard checks our identities. Another examines the objects that we deposit on a little table. The examination is meticulous, and the rules are strict. Boxer shorts yes; trousers no. T-shirts yes; shirts no. Short socks yes; long socks no. Only then are we allowed through to the visiting area. All the guards are wearing sinister black uniforms.

The visiting area has five booths. I see him sitting in one of the middle ones, on the other side of a glass partition. His face is pale and expressionless; his head has been shaved. We talk via an interphone. Few words. Obvious questions, obvious answers. "How are you?" "Do you need anything?" This isn't the time for judgements. It's about showing that when there's nothing else, there's still family. But the question on my mind is: "and afterwards?" What impression will prison leave on him? Will it be like the mark left by a branding iron? Or something like a bruise, disappearing after a short time?

Prisons are ugly places. It occurred to me that I was getting to know the Holy Land not for its beautiful landscapes and ancient temples, but for its dark spaces, through which prisoners and transgressors pass. I must ask Abou to take me to see something nice, I thought.

46.

— So doctor, could we say that we live in a world where we're all dependent on some kind of psychoactive substance? That we all have our vices?

— Yes, we're all addicts. Human beings have always needed sedatives and stimulants; that's why it's important that society understands the need of some people for narcotics, the same way others need coffee or sleeping pills.

— What is this psychic disorder that we all suffer from?

— It's a primordial pain we all carry within us. It's the angst that stems from knowing that we must die. It's the concept of innate suffering in Buddhism, the helplessness at birth that Freud talks about, the guilt for Original Sin in the Bible.

— And there's no way of escaping it?

— It's difficult. There's no other species as helpless as humans. Babies are born completely vulnerable; if they're left alone, they'll die in a matter of hours or days. This helplessness at birth never leaves us; it becomes the fear of a new helplessness. And we also suffer contingent pressures of social origin.

— How much does this affect us?

— *A great deal: just as much as physical pain. We may not always be aware of it, but we always feel a sense of incompleteness, a need to project beyond ourselves.*

— *When does drug use become a problem?*

— *When it creates a damaging behavioural dependency.*

— *What causes this dependency?*

— *An imbalance in our brain between the system of gratification, which seeks the satisfaction of our desires, and the system of regulation, which moderates them.*

— *And what causes this imbalance?*

— *In general, childhood trauma. There's a clear correlation between addiction and childhood trauma. Some people call addiction the self-medication of a trauma.*

— *And how can it be treated?*

— *Through psychoanalytic methods which reinforce behaviours resistant to desire. Psychiatry based solely on medication has proven ineffective, and the number of cases has grown exponentially. I also see countless cases of addiction which aren't necessarily extreme.*

— *But is it possible to break an addiction using methods which are fundamentally psychoanalytic?*

— *It's extremely difficult, but there's no alternative.*

— *How do you deal with your patients?*

— *I try to motivate patients to change their behaviour, without sermonising or judging them, and without assuming I know what is good or bad for them.*

— *But surely you have your own ideas?*

— *Of course, but I can't control what the patient does or doesn't do.*

— *How does that work in practice?*

— *I try to find a balance between respect for their autonomy and my own convictions.*

— *Can you give me an example?*

— *Imagine my patient is a woman who was sexually abused as a child. She's now a heroin addict who injects every six hours. Now, suppose that she's pregnant. What I try to do is help her reduce it to once a day rather than four times, if that's the best she can manage.*

— *But how can you avoid judging her irresponsible, even criminal, given that she knows she's poisoning her baby?*

— *I can't judge her choices, because her heroin use reflects her suffering, or an attempt to overcome it. What I say to her is this: you came to me because you're worried that social services will take your children away. Let's see how we can reduce that risk. What do you think about injecting just once a day, rather than four times? Could you manage it? And how about you stop sharing needles? They're practical proposals.*

— *And does it work?*

— *Temporarily, or if the addict stands to lose something very important.*

— *But the public services only treat addicts if they stop using drugs immediately.*

— *What's more, even patients who return home are submitted to weekly drug tests. If they fail, then their treatment is suspended and their financial assistance cut. This is both absurd and unethical: people seek treatment precisely because they can't control themselves.*

— *So it's wrong to make the support conditional?*

— *Absolutely.*

— *And what's the reasoning of the public services?*

— *They argue that if the addict isn't clean, then they'll spend the money they receive on drugs. It's like denying help to a diabetic because they could spend the money on sweets, or to someone with emphysema because they could buy cigarettes. It reflects a deeply ingrained moralism in our culture that considers drug addiction a lack of character.*

— *And where does this moralistic culture come from?*

— *From religious dogma, with its salvationist concepts of virtue and sin, which are completely contrary to a medical perspective. This moralism stigmatizes the addict; it others them. But this is a phenomenon that affects all of us. It has long since ceased being marginal, and it can't be isolated or kept at arm's length.*

— *What do you do when a patient relapses?*

— *I consider drug addiction to be a chronic disorder with recurrent periods of remission. There's no definitive cure. I think everyone relapses; I don't see that as a major issue.*

— *If you can't promise a cure, what have you got to offer?*

— *No-one can promise a cure.*

47.

We were staying at Abou's house, a three-storey mansion on Mount Carmel, waiting for him to be admitted into rehab. If the patient has any medical issue besides the addiction, they won't be admitted; as there was some confusion about the results of his tests, we had to wait two days before we could see a doctor again. Abou took us out walking. The Arab settlements are characterised by big three- and even four-storey houses, like that of Abou's family. From a distance, they look like hotels. Abou explained that the custom is for the head of the family to occupy one floor, and each married son another.

I was fascinated by the landscape of Galilee; it was irresistibly cinematographic. That Saturday we visited Daliat el-Carmel, the main Druze city, followed by a shrine to a Druze patriarch close to the Sea of Galilee. That was when I found out that the Druze are spiritists, just like the followers of Allan Kardec. They believe in the transmigration of the soul and reincarnation, while their branch of Islam also incorporates philosophical ideas from Plato and Aristotle. I began to suspect that Allan Kardec didn't invent anything, he just copied it from the Druze.

When we get back, he suddenly says, "Abou, I need to go to Tel Aviv, take me to the bus stop." He's curt. He doesn't say "I want"; it's "I need". It's clear that something's bothering him. I try to think what it could be, but I don't know what to ask, and so say nothing. He's walking from one side of the living room to the other like a caged animal. Fátima, Abou's wife – who is a social worker – notices the tension and takes him aside to talk. They have a conversation in a mix of Hebrew and English. I leave them to it.

But when the conversation finishes, he asks again: "Abou, take me to the bus stop." He grabs his rucksack and stands in the doorway as if to say, "If you won't take me then I'll just walk." I decide to go with him, then change my mind. There was no point in trying to watch over him. "Perhaps it's best," I say, "so you can wake up in Tel Aviv ready for your doctor's appointment." I ask Abou to take him to the bus stop and give him some change for the fare.

I don't get much sleep that night; my imagination runs riot. In the morning I get a call from Michel, his Brazilian friend in Tel Aviv. "He disappeared", he says, "He dumped his rucksack here last night, went out, and hasn't come back." I catch a bus to Tel Aviv. A nervous journey of an hour and a half. Upon arrival, I find out that he has made off with a hundred dollars belonging to his friend. What's more, I'm fretting about his doctor's appointment. If he misses it, he won't be admitted to rehab. "Where can he be?" I ask. Michel says there was no sign of him at the central bus station, which is where all the dealers and addicts hang out, like in São Paulo's Cracolândia. "Where can he be then?" I ask again. "He might be at Gat Rimon." I recognise the address from the letters we sent him. He must have lived there for a while.

"The building's abandoned, but I know a way we can get in", explains Michel. "It's close; we can go on foot." It's a large, dilapidated house on a backstreet where there's some building work going on. Michel jumps the wall with the ease of someone who's done it plenty of times and disappears. In just a few minutes he comes back. "He's up there asleep", he says.

With his help, I jump the wall. We climb a staircase covered in detritus. And there he is, asleep on a mattress, an empty bottle of vodka by his side. Before waking him, I take in the scene. It's filthy. Cigarette butts litter the floor. There's a writing desk which is falling to pieces; inside one of the drawers I find some comic books and porno mags.

48.

Drug withdrawal is terrible. With it comes the sickness, a state of total mental collapse. As they feel it approach, addicts embark on a frantic search for the psychoactive substance, to try and ward it off. This is the definitive proof of addiction. Once this limit has been reached, the addiction becomes incurable. The most common type is alcoholism. De Quincey describes it as follows: "The Drinker rises through continual ascents to a summit or apex, from which he descends through corresponding steps of declension. There is a crowning point in the movement upwards, which once attained cannot be renewed."

The most dangerous addictions are to heroin and cocaine. At the height of their delirium, addicts have been known to cut open their arms and legs because they feel that there are insects crawling around in their veins that they have to expel. Some of them try suicide. In Japanese clinics, recovering heroin addicts are monitored by judokas, and the most aggressive ones are put in cages, to stop them from killing themselves.

49.

Crystal, the doctor wrote on the form. She didn't even need to ask. She took one look at his dilated pupils. He just nodded. At the time I didn't know what crystal was, though I do now. It's a synthetic hallucinogen which can be swallowed in pill form, ground and snorted like cocaine, dissolved in water and injected, or inserted in the anus by means of a syringe. It's considered to be an aphrodisiac and popular in nightclubs as a dance drug.

That was the day I realised that it wasn't about a specific psychoactive substance. He would take whatever he could get his hands on. Oliver Sacks – who went through all of this – said that people aren't looking for a specific effect from the psychoactive substance, but rather a vague feeling of happiness. One thing I did notice, though, was that he didn't inject. Those who inject have reached the final circle of hell, mutilating their own bodies in a kind of self-flagellation. He hadn't descended to such depths.

Crystal is a type of amphetamine; the pharmaceutical industry offers a wide variety of such drugs. Ecstasy pills are popular with European teenagers. Truck drivers use Benzedrine to keep them awake on 20-hour drives, so they can make their drops on time. Students take Adderall before a night spent cramming for an exam. Amphetamines are the magic potion of our era of savage competition, of every man for himself. At high doses the user may become violent or be overcome by paranoid fantasies and hallucinations. Continuous use leads to irreversible brain damage.

Crystal, the doctor wrote on the rehabilitation admissions form. "Since when?" I asked myself.

50.

26 OCTOBER 2015

Beirut airport authorities have foiled one of the country's largest drug smuggling attempts, seizing two tons of amphetamines before they were loaded onto the private plane of a Saudi prince. Investigators said they found forty bags of Captagon amphetamine pills and some cocaine aboard the plane, which was about to depart for the northern Saudi city of Ha'il. A security source told AFP that the prince has been identified in media reports as Ahmed bin Walla bin Abdala. He and other suspects are being questioned by authorities. Captagon is the brand name for the amphetamine fenethylline, a synthetic psychostimulant mostly used in the Middle East, particularly in Syria.

51.

I watched *The Basketball Diaries* again, paying closer attention to the details. In the final scene, the mother keeps the door on the latch while her son desperately begs her to give him five dollars, the price of a hit. Equally desperate, she hesitates, but in the end slams the door in his face without giving him the money. The mother's lesson was also my lesson. The film is based on a book by Jim Carroll, a talented basketball player who became a drug addict at a very young age. He also wrote compulsively, poems and a diary, and published several books after he got clean. Going back to the film after so many years, I was struck by how much the plot corresponds to our experience. The stealing, the arrests – it's all there. The only thing I don't know is if he ever prostituted himself, and I surely never will. And I don't know whether there'll be a happy ending like in the film.

52.

To arrive at Kiryat Shlomo you need to have the directions handy. It isn't signed, nor is it visible from the highway. It's as if it were trying to hide. We crossed an orange grove, then a patch of wasteland, until we arrived at a strawberry field. Only then did we see the white building. Young men and women were bent over the rows of bushes, picking strawberries. Two men were watching them, as if standing guard.

Kiryat Shlomo is a hospital for the mentally ill. It's a three-storey building, entirely surrounded by a fence. It has two gates side by side, between which there is a high guardhouse. One of the gates leads to the hospital itself, while the other leads to Tzeadim, a drug rehabilitation clinic in the back of the building. I found out later that the young strawberry pickers were from Tzeadim.

Abou explained that *tzeadim* means "steps" in Hebrew. Such clinics in Brazil often have similar names. It's a reference to the idea of getting clean one day at a time. One step at a time. The Brazilian clinics also tend to be in the back of something else: churches, spiritist centres, government buildings. Always in the back; a strange poetics of gloomy spaces.

I found out that in Israel there are a dozen of these rehabilitation clinics. If the addict decides to seek treatment, they consult their doctor on the national health service, who puts them on a twenty-one-day detoxification process. They must be drug free to get admitted to one of the long-term treatment communities. All these phases are voluntary; the addict has to want the treatment.

As soon as Abou pulled up outside, another car arrived, out of which stepped a girl and a middle-aged man with a haggard expression, who I assumed was her father. She was blonde, petite, with wavy hair and a doll-like face. She was wearing jeans and a white top. I put her at eighteen or nineteen. She took a suitcase out of the boot, gave the man a goodbye hug, and then walked over to the gate. It looked like the porter knew her, because he opened the gate as soon as she approached, giving her a wave. Only then did I go over to the porter and explain, in English, the reason for my visit, which I had arranged on the phone beforehand. After a brief look at some papers in front of him, he opened the gate. Abou didn't come in with me.

I found him sitting with a few others, with a blank expression on his face. We didn't talk much. He introduced me to the coordinator, a Russian, with whom I talked for a few minutes in English. Then he showed me the dormitories upstairs, each of which had six beds and a bathroom with a shower. All the other installations were precarious, as if everything were there only provisionally.

I found out that lots of the patients were alcoholics, most of them immigrants from Russia and Georgia. The young people there seemed aged beyond their years. I was reminded of my wife's account of his first spell in rehab, at the clinic in Campinas. Although everyone there was only passing through, I noticed that they treated each other with affection, as if they had known each other for a long time.

I wanted to know what was going to happen once the detoxification phase finished a few days later. He had made an agreement with his doctor to enter a long-term treatment community, but would they transfer him there directly, or would someone have to take him? He had been through detox in Israel several years before, but baulked when the time came to begin the long-term treatment. And when he was sent down for six months for beating up his girlfriend, he turned down the judge's offer of a year in rehab instead. He preferred prison.

This time, my thinking was that if they transferred him directly, it would save me the trouble of having to go and pick him up. I wanted him to feel such solitude and despair as would lead him to opt for the long-term treatment that twice he had refused. But again I had lost my nerve, asking Abou to take me to see him the day before he was due to be transferred. I don't know if this was the right thing to do. I do know that it made no difference to what happened subsequently. As I was leaving he said, "After treatment I plan to go into social work with addicts." I said nothing. Everything he says is like water dripping through your fingers. The coordinator said that they would take him to the community directly. A door-to-door system. So my visit was a wasted journey. Well, not entirely, as that journey was what led me to write my letter of emancipation.

I left with an aching heart. As I passed the guardhouse, I asked the porter if he knew the girl who had entered before me. "That was Yael", he said, "It is the third or fourth time." "So many?" I asked. "Yes, it is very sad; they always return."

53.

Sometimes I picture him as a virtuoso guitarist. An artist. He didn't lack talent. He played jazz guitar with great skill. It was almost as if his long, slender fingers could make the guitar speak. Art might not have been his salvation, but it could at least have given his life some value and his addiction some pretext. For the artist, everything is permitted. Heroin flowed freely through the veins of the jazz legends, alcohol and opium through those of great painters. Poets smoked hashish for inspiration. Huxley claimed mescaline produced effects comparable to those felt by artistic geniuses and great visionaries. A whole generation of American writers hit the bottle so hard they forged a new, macho, alcoholic literary genre. But although they might serve as inspiration, drugs can be deadly. Drugs and alcohol have led dozens of artists to an early grave. He didn't have to be a Chet Baker or a Jimi Hendrix. He could simply have been a good guitarist, living from his art.

I used to send him recordings of Yamandu Costa and Duo Assad. Sometimes I'd send him a set of guitar strings. Once he asked for something by the Cuban Leo Brouwer. I went searching through the record shops, in vain. Some months later, the music department at the University of São Paulo invited Brouwer for a symposium, where I discovered that he was revered amongst classical guitar virtuosos and experts. This was at the time of the severe shortages in Cuba due to the collapse of the Soviet Union, and Brouwer didn't bring any records with him. I did send him some of Brouwer's sheet music though.

A long time passed before I went to visit him again. When I arrived, I noticed that the sixth string of his guitar was missing, the E-string. And the tuning peg was broken. "How long has it been like that?" I asked. "A year, I think." "And why don't you mend it?" He didn't respond; he shrugged his shoulders and started to fingerpick with just five strings.

There was a musical instrument shop nearby. I bought a complete set of tuning pegs and fixed the broken one with superglue. "Wait 24 hours," I told him, "and if the glue doesn't hold, then you can just replace it with a new peg. Do you have a screwdriver?" "No, but I can get one from my neighbour." I left a new set of strings with him as well. A month later, I found out he had replaced the broken tuning peg with one of the new ones. Even so, the image of the broken guitar remained forever impressed on my memory, a symbol of a wasted life.

54.

I confess that there are times when I've wanted him dead. It's a thought I've always quickly banished, scared at myself. My need for relief was so great and so urgent that I didn't consider the inconceivable suffering that losing my only son would bring. Or perhaps I thought a definitive loss would be easier to bear than the constant distress. Paradoxically, the only rest we've had in all these years was during the six months of abstinence he was forced to undergo whilst in prison for beating up his girlfriend.

I have often asked myself, what good is a son like this? If I were a believer, I would say that he came to this world to test us. He wasted all his talent. He faked all emotions. He feigned affection for his parents when he needed money, loyalty to his friends when he needed shelter. Sooner or later, everyone abandons him. They get on with their lives and cast him off like a piece of debris. He became so insignificant that if he had suddenly ceased to exist, only us, his parents, would have noticed. Life can take many forms, and it's always possible to change its form. But our time is limited. Half his time has already gone. That's why I ask myself, what good is a son like this?

55.

In an enclave in the mountains of Gilboa, far from any town or settlement and almost entirely surrounded by the territory of the Palestinian National Authority, lies the community of Malkishua, which is where he finally went into rehab. Malkishua is the most remote of Israel's rehabilitation communities. Beyond it, there's nothing. Just barbed wire fences and a strip of no man's land.

Before I went back to Brazil I asked Abou to take me to see him. It's a long journey, as you have to skirt around all of Palestinian Jenin. It oozes history from start to finish. It begins at the Megiddo Junction, where the Battle of Megiddo between the Egyptians and the Canaanites took place in 1500 BC Abou took me to a small museum there, built around a well sunk by the Canaanites, which pays tribute to the famous battle.

From Megiddo the road crosses the Jezreel Valley, where the first Jewish immigrants of the modern era settled 140 years ago. At that time Jezreel was an inhospitable, malaria-ridden swamp. The Arab population in the whole of Palestine was less than half a million. Today, the valley is home to fields of corn and wheat, as well as Jewish collective farms. The Jewish population is more than seven million; the Arabs are nearly two million just in Israel, where they suffer discrimination, and another five million in the territory of the Palestinian National Authority and scattered around the world. We tell the story of their dramatic exile in our documentary.

When you reach the Gilboa foothills, the road narrows, snaking around the hillside, rising and falling endlessly. In these craggy mountains, Saul, the first King of Israel, defeated the Philistines in 2000 BC. We looked out over the valley from a viewpoint at the top of the hill. It was yellowish in colour and dotted with fish breeding ponds that reflected the sunlight like little mirrors. The view is spectacular. Further away, you can see the irregular green streak of the River Jordan against the stark sepia background of the mountains of Jordan. To the south you can see Nazareth, where Jesus Christ was raised. Druze and Bedouin settlements can be seen to the west. Although the Druze practice their own religion, Abou seemed to know the Christian shrines well and described them in detail.

Beforehand, we had consulted the Malkishua website. The community has three different rehabilitation centres: one for adolescents, one for adults, and one for religious young people. All are under the control of the Ministry of Health. Treatment takes a year and a half, the time considered necessary to change the addict's behaviour. It involves four stages of decreasing intensity: three within the community, and the final one outside, under supervision in urban residences.

A little before reaching the gate of the community, we were surprised by a lush vineyard, which followed the curves of a gully between the mountains. It was the only crop we had seen during the whole journey; perhaps it belonged to the community itself. When we finally arrived, it was as silent as a convent. For nearly ten minutes, nobody came to attend to us. When two shaven-headed young men carrying a bucket passed us, Abou asked them in Hebrew where the reception was. They didn't respond. They seemed scared, making a gesture with their heads which I later realised meant that they were forbidden to speak.

He appeared a few minutes later, with his head shaved, a rigid posture, and a scared expression on his face. He talked of a system of punishment and mentioned someone who had recently dropped out. He also said that of the group who had enrolled a year ago, only four of them had stuck with it. That was all he said. It was brief. He had begun to think about leaving soon after he had entered. "For as long as you're getting treatment, you can count on my support", I told him. "If you give up, forget that you have a father." And I left. As we began the return journey, I initially regretted having been so tough with him when he was looking so down. I got this off my chest with Abou, who said nothing. Two weeks later, after I had returned to Brazil, I phoned Malkishua to find out how he was doing. "He left us", said the secretary drily. That same day I wrote the letter.

56.

I can't finish without mentioning our own deceptions, though they were innocent when compared with his, starting with the unofficial adoption, without going through the family courts. We've always told him that we don't know who his biological parents are, and this is the truth. The woman who brought us the baby told us that she didn't know. We've never told him clearly who that woman was and how we met her. It never occurred to us that it might be important, and as time went by it all was forgotten.

On the question of his biological mother, we simply kept quiet. We've never referred to her negatively, nor in any other way. But silence can also produce meaning – or worse, intense speculation. To the contrary of what we thought, this only became more powerful, haunting the imagination of the adopted child.

Today I know that children need the truth to organise their world, but they don't ask questions they feel their parents might have difficulty answering. He didn't ask. But for a child who has been adopted unofficially, the truth is even more important. He was at an even greater disadvantage than an orphan, because he doesn't know who his parents, grandparents, aunts, and uncles were. Without this information, it's hard to structure oneself as a subject. The individual may end up insecure, more likely to seek spiritual peace in the artificial paradise.

I've also learnt that having a frank discussion about the adoption – with the right words and at the right time – is crucial in the formation of the emotional bond. I don't know whether we did this well or not. I've read that in France, a mother who gives up her child has to leave them a letter explaining her reasons. I can only wonder what he thought when he became conscious of the fact that he was adopted. Or worse, what he might have thought in adolescence, after becoming aware of the darker side of life. Was he the product of a rape, or incest? Perhaps he took refuge in an idealized vision of a biological mother who was simply very poor or incapacitated. Perhaps.

A doctor friend of ours wrote a certificate declaring he had been born at home. With this fraudulent document, we obtained a birth certificate which said he was our biological child, as well as his school enrolments and his vaccination record. All of it false by association. As an adult he obtained his ID card, his employment record, and his passport in the same way. My friend Leopold got a declaration of Jewish heritage from a rabbi, based on my wife's papers, though as she was his adoptive mother he had no Jewish blood. That was another lie. So there was a lot of deceit. I'm a worrier by nature, and for a long time I was scared we would be exposed. Not my wife though. She was never concerned. For her, this was simply the subterfuge inherent to any adoption, whether done officially or not.

57.

I thought I had finished this account, and then I dreamt of him. As soon as I woke up, I wrote it down. Dreams are manifestations of desire or anxiety. There's something which has been bothering me. Something related to this account. It was a long dream, composed of distinct scenes like a film. In the first, I'm just a spectator. I see him somewhere in Israel, with a Palestinian who has a truck with a large closed body. He's just helping. He looks good, wholesome. A little clumsy, a bit slow in the head, but good natured. The Palestinian has my Lebanese grandfather's face. The side doors of the lorry are open, and inside I can see the carcass of an ox, like those that meat-packing plants send to the butcher's to be cut up. The Palestinian is bragging about having bought the meat for just a thousand dollars, when they can sell it for a million. "We're going to make a million!" he shouts. "A million!" In the next scene, he and the Palestinian are dragging the carcass on a string out in the desert somewhere, where they both dig a hole in which to bury it. "*Yala! Yala!*" the Palestinian is shouting. "Quickly! Quickly!" Exactly like my grandfather used to shout when he got impatient. The meat has gone bad, everything has gone wrong, but neither of them seems much to care. In the language of dreams, holes and hollow spaces can represent the female genitalia or maternity. In the dream there's a double hollow: the open lorry, and inside it the carcass, which is also open. It could be interpreted as a double maternity, the biological mother and the adoptive mother. By burying the carcass, he buries one of them. But which one? As he's calm in the scene, I suppose that he's burying the mother who gave him up, and with it, overcoming the trauma of the adoption. But then I'm the one who's dreaming. I'm the one who wants him to get over his trauma. And the Palestinian? Why is he shouting that he's going to make a million? The million recalled the income tax declaration that I had just completed, requiring me to confirm that my assets were worth a million. The Palestinian in the dream is, therefore, me, the grandchild of Arabs, declaring that my assets are worth a million, which will be his when I die. In the following scene we're both in a courtroom, waiting for the verdict on a case he has brought against someone who stole his mobile phone. He's standing, examining a row of three green plastic chairs, as if wondering whether to sit down. The green chairs could represent the green of *Cannabis sativa*, which I don't want him to succumb to. I ask him why the mobile phone is so important. "I don't care about the phone itself", he says, "It's about what's recorded on it. I don't want the thief to listen to it." I suppose that the recordings represent the content of this story. I'm the thief. I went rooting in his diary, I stole his story and turned it into a book. The dream expresses my fear that he'll react badly to what I've written, that he'll repudiate me if I publish, just as I've repudiated him for the actions I've described. Then there's a sequence where he's travelling with a merry group of young people on the back of a truck that has to skirt around the Sea of Galilee, which has flooded. A full lake suggests drowning. Having the truck skirt around the lake is a manifestation of my wish that he escape his addiction. Then the same young people dance on a stage while he looks on, leaning against a low wall. There's a girl there, wearing a tight top which shows off her voluptuous breasts, dancing with a short guy. He goes over and asks her if she wants to carry on dancing, or if she'd prefer to go back to his place to have sex. She chooses the latter. Then they're outside his room. When he opens the door, the room is full of smoke and there are three boys inside. Two of them are asleep, and the other is sitting on a chair, playing the guitar. The girl is amused by this and the two of them give up on the idea of sex. I have no idea about the dancing scene. But the smoky room, which they don't enter, expresses my desire that he abandon the world of drug addiction. In the next scene, the last one, I feature again. He turns to me and says, with an air of satisfaction, that he's receiving a pension of a thousand dollars a month. "What pension?" I ask. "It's a pension that the Israeli government gives to people who have come from countries where there's a lot of violence." I do some mental calculations, trying to work out whether a thousand dollars a month is enough to live on in Israel. I decide not, though I don't say anything. He opens an envelope. "Look, I'm saving up", he says, showing me four or five brown cheques for a thousand dollars. And then he adds something which surprises me even in the dream: "Dad, why don't you come over here as well and live off this money?" The envelope represents the letter with which I began this account. The letter with which I banished him from my presence. His invitation to join him represents my guilt for having done so.

In previous dreams he had always appeared as a small child, just four or five years old, playful, happy, as he was at that age. Those dreams I interpreted as the expression of a nostalgic desire for him to have turned out differently. In this dream, he appears as an adult, a young man of around twenty-five, tall, a little skinny, but all in all looking very well. Perhaps it's just the same desire expressed a different way.

127

Postscript

Two years went by and we heard nothing from him. Two painful years in which we made an enormous effort to forget him. Until one night, the phone rang. It was him. He spoke to his mother. He sounded tired, she told me later. Sleepy, but calm. He told her that he was working as a sous-chef in a tourist resort called Aqaba, in the south of Jordan, on the shore of the Red Sea. And he was well. He said that after leaving Malkishua, with nowhere to stay and no money, he had got a job on an Italian merchant ship at Haifa as they needed someone urgently to work in the galley. He said that in Jordan people don't drink alcohol, they're more polite than in Israel, and that almost everyone speaks English. He assured us he was clean. "I'm fine", he repeated several times. And he told us not to worry.

How were we supposed not to worry? Immediately, it all began again. The same anxiety. The same doubts. Was he really fine, or just pretending? Why had he called? Why now? Did he want money?

Gradually the calls to his mother became more frequent, until he was calling nearly every day. Although he always assured us he was fine, it only took a couple of days without a call for the old feelings of dread and the sleepless nights to return. He had come back into our lives with the same dramatic weight as before.

Then he began exchanging messages with his mother via WhatsApp. "Why doesn't Dad want to talk to me?" he complained. My wife passed me the phone and I said hello, a little curtly, perhaps wary of what my own hurt feelings might make me say if the conversation were to go on for long. But I ended up saying hello to him whenever he called his mother and I was around, less curtly, though I always held something back.

I took a lot of convincing that he really was well. After one of his phone calls, I did the maths: if he was telling the truth, then he'd have been clean for 18 months. The experts on the subject say that at least two years of abstinence are required before one can even begin to hope that there will be no relapse. Even then, the risk is always there. Abandoned to his fate, without his father or mother, without the girl who loved him, face to face with the ruin of nearly half his life – only then did he find the strength to free himself, I thought. Could it really be true? Could it be possible?

Parents can tell a lot from the tone of their children's voices. During these calls he always sounded well, sober, if a little drowsy sometimes – but then there was a five-hour time difference and he was calling in the middle of the night. And there were other positive signs. He never once mentioned money, and he was always either tired, coming in from work, or just heading out to work. He complained of the long hours and especially the night shifts, which he said he hated.

One night, however, his voice sounded dangerously melancholic. Though he insisted that he was okay, he admitted that he was lonely. He thought he was depressed. That was enough to set the alarm bells ringing. So we decided to visit. Another reason was that we'd become conscious of our own fragility in that interim; an awareness of our own mortality had taken hold of us. We'd been to a lot of funerals in those two years. My generation was coming to an end. We thought it was important for him to know this. Not to awaken his sympathy, but to give him greater strength. To make him realise that time was running out, not only for him, but also for his mother and me. And that there was little time to reconcile, to find together a loving way of life that worked for us.

I looked up Jordan and Aqaba on Google. UNESCO had just designated Petra, the ancient capital of the Nabataeans, a World Heritage Site. It's located between Amman, Jordan's capital, where the international flights landed, and Aqaba. So we decided first to do some tourism in Petra and then go on to Aqaba, as if to approach him only gradually, scouting out the terrain and preparing our spirits.

In Amman I rented a car and we stayed the night. Between Amman and Petra there are two hundred and fifty kilometres of desert, and from Petra to Aqaba another hundred and fifty. We arrived in Petra, located in a gorge between rusty-coloured mountains, at the end of a morning of intense sun. Unlike other ancient ruins, the Nabataean temples are vast caverns sculpted out of the sandstone mountains, decorated with Greco-Roman relief columns.

Petra was stunning, but our thoughts were completely dominated by the meeting ahead of us in Aqaba. Exhausted from the journey and the temple visits, we stayed overnight in a small boutique hotel full of rowdy English tourists. In spite of the noise, I drifted off before my wife and fell into a heavy sleep, which I was glad for.

We left for Aqaba in the morning, shortly after breakfast. I drove, absorbed in my own memories, exchanging few words with my wife, who seemed to be going through something similar. Between Petra and Aqaba the landscape is intensely dry. Lots of stark, brownish mountains. I had read online that Aqaba grew out of the spice trade, the goods brought by boat from India to the Red Sea. Then the merchants continued on camels to Gaza, from where they headed to Europe across the sea; or they went to Petra en route to Damascus.

Today, Aqaba is a tourist destination for Europeans fleeing from winter. We found ourselves in a bay ringed with luxury hotels. There were people of all physical types in the streets: blacks, Arabs, blondes, Asians. I found out later that the hotels offer accommodation to their employees, which attracts all sorts: the desperate, the poor, and those of whom one tends not to ask too many questions. A kind of foreign legion. This curious backwater was where we found him.

My first impression was that he had grown. He seemed much taller than before. No. It was me who had shrunk. No-one grows after the age of 20, and he was now 37. He gave his mother a lengthy embrace, then me. I noticed that he wasn't sniffing, nor was he touching his nose with his finger every few minutes, like he had been the last time we saw him.

He seemed just as loquacious as ever. He talked in a loud voice, gesticulating, his words gushing out continuously as if to leave no space for doubts or replies, his tone slightly theatrical, as if to conceal insecurity. But his face, which had been disdainful, almost defiant, was different: focused, guarded. Likewise, what he said was dense, logical, mature. He surprised me.

He explained that on the Italian boat they paid him a pittance and conditions were terrible, so he left as soon as they moored in Aqaba. At the hotel he had accommodation and the wages were a little better than on the boat, but he had no money to spare as he was paying off his debts. I was stunned. I remembered that when we cut ties with him, I'd told him that if one day he decided to sort himself out, he could start by paying back all the money he had taken from his friends. But I said nothing about it. "I've paid Karl back," he said, "Abou as well." And by the end of the year he said he would have paid back Michel, the friend he lived with in Tel Aviv.

We went for lunch together. He ordered prawns, which reminded me of his refined tastes and behaviour at the table. He'd always liked prawns. It also occurred to me that he must not have much money and was making the most of the fact that we were paying. I don't mean that in a bad way; to the contrary, I was glad to give him that pleasure. Between mouthfuls, he explained in great detail how the hotel worked, how much he earned and how much was left over after they had subtracted his bed and board. He talked about the bosses, his colleagues, what they were like. He was alert, on top of everything that was going on. Perhaps overly concerned with small details, I even thought.

But he soon began to talk about abstract topics. He said he was still a spiritist, but not in the same way as before. His vision of spiritism had changed. The way he said this was so beautiful that I forced myself to memorize it. Later on I wrote it down, to make sure I didn't forget. It was this: "From spiritism I took the moral teachings about conduct, about family, about the need for perfection of the spirit, but spiritism doesn't explain the workings of our mind, nor the relationship between thought and emotion. I found this in Buddhism. I don't think about life after death any more, nor about reincarnation. I think about the life I'm living, about who I am and who I want to be. I'm looking for self-knowledge, the true nature of things."

I had brought him the book *Emotional Intelligence* by Daniel Goleman, which he had requested. Only after this declaration of his principles did I understand the enthusiasm with which he thanked me for it. It seemed clear to me that he had built a mental framework for himself, to help him reorganize a life which had hitherto had no direction.

Later that day, on the way to the restaurant where we were to have dinner, he began to ask us about the adoption. Who was the woman who gave him to us? Where did she live? What was her name? Why did we say that it was an *adoção à brasileira*? Did we mean it was illegal? How was he registered? "A doctor friend of ours declared that you were born at home", I told him. I let his mother deal with the other questions.

His questions weren't angry, but they were firm. I realised that it wasn't just curiosity; it was the search for self-knowledge for which only now was he prepared, whatever the responses might be. Had we ever said the words "illegal adoption", I wondered? If we had, then it had been a grave mistake. Would that make him illegal? Would it mean he was in the world illegally? My wife reassured me afterwards that we had never said anything of the sort.

He also wanted to know about the plaster, the boots, how long all of that lasted. Then he began asking about his friends, starting with the oldest ones, from when he was still in preschool. He wanted to know how they all were and what they were doing, commenting on all of them.

There were two moments which scared me. The first was when he said that he used to hear voices, though not so much any more. The second was when, completely unprompted, he began talking about addicts who inject. "There are a lot of addicts here as well," he said, "some of them even shoot up. Why is it that people don't shoot up in Brazil? It's an American thing." Then he concluded: "The most dangerous thing is to get fucked up in the head."

"Michel's in a bad way", he said then. We were surprised, because it had always been Michel who came to his rescue in his worst moments. "It's just that he manages to stay on top of it, pay his rent, and he has the motorbike, so he can get to work." I noticed that he was talking about addicts and even about Michel as if they were other. He was putting them at a distance, reiterating for his own benefit and for ours that he had left that world.

The next day he showed us his little room in the residential block for the hotel employees. Until just a few days previously he had been sharing it with an Arab from Amman, the son of Palestinians who had been expelled from their village by Jewish settlers in the war of 1948. He explained that the Arab had come to Aqaba after his wife had left him. He had gone back to Amman following a call from his mother, who had found him another wife. He said he had been getting on well with him, though he resented the lack of privacy. In a few days someone else would come and occupy the empty bed. There were two employees in every room, forced to coexist.

The room recalled the cell of a prisoner who had not allowed himself to become despondent, nor lose his humanity. A prisoner with their self-esteem intact, determined to recover their freedom and a functional life. The bed was made, the floor clean. Everything neat and tidy. Every object in its right place, suggesting a mind equally organised.

There was no trace of the dirt and squalor that I had seen in the kitchenette he shared with Michel and the others in Tel Aviv. The monastic nature of his room, along with his exhausting shifts at work, gave the impression that he was a penitent. He was fulfilling a promise he had made to himself.

He stripped down to his boxers and got changed in front of us, without any embarrassment. It was an interesting moment, because the absence of modesty showed us that he was still our son, the child whom we had bathed and who used to sit on our laps. I saw that he was skinnier than ever. His was a lean body, of a mixed-race complexion. But he had no muscle mass or excess fat. I felt really sorry for him; I wanted to help.

We stayed in Aqaba for three days. On the last day he said that he didn't understand how he had ended up there, but that everything he had been through had been necessary for him to find himself. He said he was doing a lot of reading online – Brazilian, American and English books; they were helping him to think. He said recently he had been feeling good alone, even enjoying it. "I've changed a lot as a person", he said. "I think a lot and I'm at peace with myself."

He cried when we left. We thought about leaving him some money, as a sign of affection and to relieve his penury, but we decided that intervening in the delicate financial balance he had found might have negative consequences for his spiritual balance.

When we were in the car ready to leave, he came up to the window and gripped his mother's arm. "You know, Mum, I asked you all those questions, but I never had a problem with the adoption, because our spirits already knew each other from before", he said. "You were always my mum. When we used to walk around hand in hand and other people would talk about us, I couldn't understand it."

This is where I finish. We went back to Brazil with our fingers crossed.

Latin America Bureau (LAB)

Latin America Bureau (Research and Action) Limited (LAB) is an independent, non-profit publishing and research organization based in the UK. A registered charity, LAB provides news, analysis and information on Latin America, reporting consistently from the perspective of the region's social movements and poor, oppressed or marginalized communities – aiming to convey their voices to a wide readership across the English-speaking world.

Founded in 1977, LAB has published over 150 books and operates a lively website (www.lab.org.uk) and Facebook page (https://www.facebook.com/latinamericabureau/). You can sign up to receive the newsletter by clicking 'Subscribe' on the www.lab.org.uk home page.

Practical Action Publishing Ltd distribute all LAB titles, new and old. You can see the full catalogue at https://developmentbookshop.com/latin-america-bureau-titles. As well as print books, many titles are available in digital form and educational institutions can subscribe to individual chapters for course reading lists.

For more information, email contactlab@lab.org.uk

K
By Bernardo Kucinski

Bernardo Kucinski

K is the story of a father who searches desperately for his daughter, 'disappeared' during the military dictatorship in Brazil. The father is himself a refugee from Poland in the 1930s. He is racked by feelings of guilt—that because he was immersed in his Yiddish writing and scholarship, he did not really know his daughter or the danger that threatened her. The novel is based on a true story – the disappearance of Kucinski's younger sister in 1973. As the author says, 'Everything in this book is invented but almost everything happened'.

Published by LAB, in partnership with Practical Action Publishing.